MEDALLION STATUS

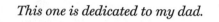

This one is dedicated to my dad.

Thank you for being OK with me having so many weird jobs.

Contents

1 | **OBLIGATORY MAINE CONTENT**   1

2 | **NUDE RIDER**   4

3 | **THANK YOU FOR BEING GOLD**   19

4 | **SECRET FAMILY**   31

5 | **RACKING UP MILES**   50

6 | **THE SPORT OF MARBLE KINGS**   74

7 | **DISNEY JAIL**   91

8 | **SECRET SOCIETY**   105

9 | **CAREER ADVICE FOR CHILDREN**   122

10 | **AWARDS SEASON**   152

11 | BELOVED ONE 167

12 | JONATHAN AND DREW AND
LINUS AND CHOMPERS 175

13 | A GREAT WAY TO RUIN A DIAMOND 193

14 | THIS WAS ALL OPTIONAL 200

15 | TIPS TO ACE YOUR AUDITION 212

16 | A PARABLE 217

17 | ALL I DO IS WIN 222

18 | TWO BUILDINGS IN FLORIDA 237

19 | A MAN GOES ON A JOURNEY 260

20 | A STRANGER COMES TO TOWN 265

Acknowledgments 287

I've seen things you people wouldn't believe. Attack ships on fire off the shoulder of Orion. I watched C-beams glitter in the dark near the Tannhäuser Gate. All those moments will be lost in time, like tears in rain.

ROY BATTY

To everyone who's ever been on television, cling to it. As long as you can.

JON STEWART

I hereby confirm that, in accordance with Section 43.A. of the Producer-Screen Actors Guild Codified Basic Agreement ("SAG Agreement"), as amended from time to time, you have notified me of the nude scene expected to be performed by me in the above Role for episode #108 of the Program (the "Episode") for which I am engaged.

JOHN HODGMAN

MEDALLION STATUS

Chapter One

OBLIGATORY MAINE CONTENT

I f you read my previous book you know that I spend part of the year with my family in an unnamed coastal town in Maine. Of course the town *has* a name. I just kept it secret. But some of you figured it out anyway. Some of you sent me some very nice letters and postcards at my post office box there (PO Box 117, Unnamed Coastal Town, Maine, Zip Code Redacted). But none of you sent me creepy things, like boxes of moths, and none of you came to invade my home. So I can't write *that* book, unfortunately: the true story of you invading my home. That one would have been a huge bestseller. Now I have to write this one instead.

However, one young pair of John Hodgman fans did come to town. A nice young man and woman, plus their baby. They said they weren't there *precisely* to see me, but they had read my book and were passing through town because of it. "It's John Hodgman!" they said, in that way I've heard before when people recognize me—that up-tilting mix of surprise and familiarity, as if to say: *You exist! You're not just a television ghost, but a real person, and here you are outside the library, in a fight with your wife!*

My wife and I were fighting because we had just discovered that the passenger footwell of our Jeep had flooded with a hot reddish liquid. It was seeping into the footwell from unknown engine holes. (I don't know a lot about cars.) It smelled like burning tin foil and looked like blood and lymph, and I was freaking out.

"Just *call* Libby and tell her we can't watch her children today, because we are afraid our Jeep is maybe bleeding to death," I was saying to my wife, loudly. *"That is very reasonable!"*

I was speaking with the kind of shameful sharpness that gets in my voice when I know I am powerless. If you had told me that in fact the heater core had failed and the Jeep blood was in fact engine coolant, it would have sounded equally supernatural to me, dangerous and unsolvable. I also knew my argument was futile. Our friend Libby has two little children, a boy and a girl, who are very cute. As our own children have aged, my wife has become addicted to these other children. They are among the select group of young children that she follows on Instagram. That's what you need to know, parents who post pictures of their children on Instagram. My wife is stalking them. The Jeep could explode and she would find a way to get over to Libby's and take care of them.

That's when the young couple approached us. They said, "It's John Hodgman!" and then instantly regretted it, once they saw the panic and shame on my face.

"Yes, it's me," I said. "I'm sorry."

They accepted my apology, and we chatted. I don't remember the young man's story, but the young woman apparently had created an illustration of me for an article in a newspaper that I also don't remember. Also I don't remember their names. My wife and I admired their baby, which was one of the cuter babies (not all babies are cute. Sorry, babies). They asked about the house in town where the Famous Author had lived, and I told them that it has a new owner. I happily revealed its secret location to them. As you'll see in this book, there are no secrets anymore.

(If you don't know what Famous Author or house I'm talking about, just read my previous book, *Vacationland*. There, I tricked you into buying it.)

I was glad to talk to them. I enjoy being seen and recognized. So many people go through life without being seen at all, not even by their own family, so I know what a gift it is. And frankly it doesn't happen often these days, as I am not on television that much anymore. So if the young couple are reading this, this is to say thank you. I'm sorry I do not remember your names or where you published that illustration. I was pretty high on engine coolant at the time.

And if *you* are reading this, thank you, too. This story is not an invitation to come see me in Maine. I still prefer that you stay away. But thank you for letting me know I can trust you.

There will be no more Maine content in this book.

Chapter Two

NUDE RIDER

Not long ago I was still on television sometimes. I was appearing on *The Daily Show with Jon Stewart* less and less frequently, but I had a lot of guest-acting gigs on some prestigious shows. I played a variety of mustache creeps: a scheming literary rival; a deranged fan who claims he legally owns an actress whom he has been stalking; an evil FBI agent who interrogates a beautiful young woman and makes her cry; a psychiatrist who pulls his patients' teeth from their heads because he thinks insanity lives in the gums. He also pulls out the teeth of his own children.

For a while, this typecasting bothered me, and I fought against it. I refused the role, for example, of a man who keeps pregnant women in his basement so he can sell their babies. This role was very upsetting, in part because it had been a straight offer to me. The producers didn't even need me to audition to know that I was *just right*, the perfect person to keep women imprisoned in his basement. And apparently they were correct. I *was* the perfect person, because after I turned them down, the movie fell apart.

I didn't have to audition for the evil FBI agent either. You have probably seen that show. It's the one where a woman with a lot of tattoos turns up naked in a bag in Times Square. The woman has amnesia, and no one knows who she is. But she has a large tattoo of a name on her back, the name of the handsome FBI agent who is the other star of the show. This FBI agent is not evil. He is a nice man played by an Australian actor. He has no idea why his name is tattooed on this random amnesiac woman's back. He doesn't know her name or history any more than she does. But because he likes the tattooed woman, and because she punches and kicks good, the FBI says, *Welp, let's go ahead and make her an honorary member of this elite law enforcement agency that people train for years to become a part of. Why not?*

(Part of my evil FBI agent's motivation was that this office of the FBI was handling its hiring practices a little . . . haphazardly. And honestly, my guy had a point.)

When I was cast as the evil FBI agent, I had to shave my beard and get a new haircut. The hair-and-makeup man who cut my hair was named Craig. He asked me if there was anything he needed to know about my hair.

"Yes, Craig," I said. "My hair is extremely fine and limp, and my face is very pale and round, especially when I only have a mustache. One thing I've learned is that, unless you square off my haircut and use a lot of product to give it lift, my hair just flops forward over my forehead, and let's just say it gets pretty Hitler-y. Pretty fast."

"Got it," said Craig. And he cut my hair and styled it. And when he was done, I looked like Hitler.

"Don't you think I look like Hitler?" I asked.

"Not at all," said Craig. "You look great."

Then I went to the fake interrogation room to pretend to yell at the beautiful young woman. This was not the tattooed woman, but her friend. The interrogation room had a one-way mirror in it, and from time to time I would catch myself in it and get mad. *Ugh*, I would think. *Look at Hitler over there, yelling at that nice woman.* Between takes I would finger-comb my hair back to try to de-Hitlerize it a little. Then Craig would just sneak up behind me before the cameras rolled and re-Hitlerize it.

"You don't look like Hitler!" he would whisper as he finished. I don't know why he was doing this to me.

One nice thing about this job was that it filmed only twenty minutes from my home in Brooklyn. Every morning I would drive myself in and park, go inside, do my work, and then drive home again, just like a straight-up dad. It was wonderful.

One evening, I dropped my car off at the garage near our apartment. The garage attendant, Patrick, smiled and said, "Hey! You look like Hitler!"

"Thank you!" I said, improbably. "That's what I've been trying to tell everyone!"

He looked me over again and laughed. "You really do look just like Hitler!"

OK, now wait a minute, I wanted to say. *I don't look just like Hitler. I mean, Hitler did not wear eyeglasses. And Hitler also had a pretty specific mustache, which is not like my mustache at all. And why are you telling me a* second time*? The first time you said I looked like Hitler, it might have been out of surprise. You might have been trying to warn me of something I didn't know. But now you know I* do *know, and you're making me feel bad. You know that this is a tipping relationship, right? I give you a gift every Christmas, so maybe just, as a good business practice,* don't *compare me to one of the great monsters in history?*

Of course I tipped him—extra, in fact. I wanted to thank him for being honest and confirming that Craig was gaslighting me all along. And also, even when you're only a little bit famous you have to be generous. You don't want the garage attendant going behind your back saying that Hitler stiffed him.

My time on the show was short. Eventually the tattooed woman tired of me being mean to her friend and shot my character in the chest. I thought that meant the show had to be canceled, but no. Somehow, the show went on without me, and it is now a big success.

I was very sad that they killed me. I liked my friends on the show, and I liked my commute. It seemed to me that my exit from the show didn't have to be so final. I could come back somehow. Many other characters on the show who have died later came back as flashbacks, or hallucinations. The creator of the show is a friend of mine, and from time to time I would text him different scenarios in which they could bring Inspector Hitler back.

For example, I wrote, what if my character had been wearing a bulletproof vest, and I didn't die after all, and when the Australian FBI agent finds me on the ground, he is just a little too... you know, *Australian*... to tell the difference?

Another idea. What if the tattooed woman who shot me had *dreamed the whole thing*? What if, like, there's a scene where she's in the shower, and she glances into her armpit and says, "That's weird. There's a tattoo in my armpit that I never noticed before. It's a tattoo of me shooting John Hodgman in the chest." And that meta-tattoo proves to her that the whole event is a false memory, implanted in her mind by a mysterious secret organization dedicated to me being alive and still on television shows?

Or how about this: What if my character has a twin brother, only this one doesn't have a Hitler haircut, and he doesn't want to do anything evil or bad because he's a really good guy. And even though I don't have any training in law enforcement, and I didn't go to the FBI academy, and I wasn't even found in a bag in Times Square or anything, they let me in the FBI anyway. They make me an FBI Series Regular, which is not technically a real FBI term, but certainly is better than "FBI Guest Star" when it comes to TV residuals. I would be my own reverse-evil-twin good guy and I would join the good guy squad and solve crimes and be liked for once. The creator enjoyed these scenarios, and he told me they would never, ever happen.

One time, however, I got a break. I was cast as a charming

older mentor to a young woman. The woman was an aspiring classical oboist. My character was eccentric, but for once I was not a pure monster. I enjoyed it. I felt like I was getting away with something.

I was going to be in two episodes of the show. In my first episode, the Beautiful Oboist and I were to meet at a party in a mansion. We are there for a fund-raising event for a symphony orchestra, a stuffy society party that unwinds into genteel depravity over the course of the episode and ends up lasting until dawn.

When I read the script, the Director told me that we would not be shooting the episode in the traditional way, in bits and pieces out of chronological order. He would be shooting the episode in a series of long, real-time shots. The entire extended cast, along with dozens of background actors, would be assembled in an actual mansion on Long Island. We would pretend to have a party as the camera crew drifted in and among us, filming the important parts discreetly, like a documentary, all night long.

Even though the whiskey was apple juice and I was told not to eat the canapés, this was my kind of party. I never had to think about where to stand or what to do—that was all decided for me. And if I wanted to talk to someone, that person *had* to talk back to me because it was in the script, and they were filming my every word like I mattered. For a shy narcissist, this was a good time.

All the actors were extremely skilled and attractive and

dressed beautifully. Also, I was there. I was, arguably, one of them. The Director had loaned me his own canary yellow linen shirt to wear beneath my dinner jacket. When I put it on, I could not stop smiling. I felt like a younger brother wearing his older brother's shirt to prom. Better, actually. I was wearing his shirt to the beautiful, nice-person acting party I felt I had been crashing since the first time I was ever on television. But this time I was invited.

My character was supposed to be the weirdo bachelor heir to an obscure fortune who was now happily swanning around the arts world. Early in the party, the Beautiful Oboist and I strike up a conversation in a dining room with pictures of horses on the wall. The Beautiful Oboist confesses she is worried about whether she should continue as an oboist, and I offer her life advice. We talk and wander throughout the evening as the rest of the party's storylines unfold, watching as the show's main character is challenged to play the violin, discovering teenagers in a secret room prepping a bunch of fireworks as a prank. As per Chekhov, the fireworks went off at some point, and as the party scattered in terror, the Beautiful Oboist and I grabbed hands and ran laughing through a colonnade of trees.

When you actually stay up all night with people for three nights, it doesn't matter that you are *pretending* that you're staying up all night with them. A bond forms. You realize that that *is* a real white horse wandering around the patio, that that woman is *actually* singing a Billie Holiday song at actual dawn, and that that actor is *really* playing soccer on the lawn with the background artists posing as waiters and they are all really good at it. Fireworks are fireworks, and when you are running from them, it is hard to not feel in love. There was just enough of a spark between our characters to feel real and to make the audience worry that this young woman was going to fall for this old creep. But they didn't have to worry. For once my character was *not* a creep. He was sexless, somewhat clueless to context, and only hoping to help. It was the role of my life.

We ran from the fireworks to the actual pool by the actual mansion. It was fall, and wisps of steam were rising from the surface of the heated water. The Beautiful Oboist told me why she started playing the oboe. She worried she had chosen it just because it looked nice.

Now, I never played the oboe in high school. I had been a clarinet player—just a simple, single-reed guy. But I had enough general experience with feeling like an impostor that I could reassure her.

"No," I told her. "It's more than that."

I explained that when she chose the oboe, she had invented herself. That didn't make her an impostor. That made her brave. And we took our champagne flutes and sat down in patio chairs under the stars, and I did not spill my champagne or fall off my patio chair while doing so. I felt like I was doing a really good job at acting. When I was done, I drove myself home and had a tuna sandwich at 5 a.m. and slept well.

Then a few days after we finished filming, I received the script for my second episode. It turned out that *my* character, at least, *was* an impostor, and all the wise life advice I had offered the Beautiful Oboist in the previous episode was part of a deception. It turned out I was just trying to trick this young woman into having sex with me. In the next episode, I would come to her apartment under the premise of taking an oboe lesson. I would bring an expensive oboe with golden keys to learn on. I would honk out a few notes and then I would excuse myself to use the bathroom. But instead of using the bathroom, I would, unnervingly, start taking a shower. Then the Beautiful Oboist would discover me in her bed, completely nude, except for the oboe. Welcome back, mustache creep.

One consolation for playing all these monsters was the swag. I had collected a small hoard of swag: gifts, branded with shows' names, usually handed out to the cast at the end of production. There was my *Bored to Death* season 3 Patagonia rain jacket. My *Delocated* series finale gray hoodie. My HankCo. winter hat from *The Venture Bros.* I got my *Daily Show: Indecision 2010* zippy sweatshirt at the massive rally Jon Stewart held on the Washington Mall that year. I wasn't asked to go onstage at that event, but I did get to wear my zippy backstage while watching Kareem Abdul-Jabbar try to get out of a conversation with Tony Bennett, and then later while staying up all night with Adam Savage of *MythBusters*. Me and zippy, we could drop a lot of names, let me tell you.

There were other kinds of swag, stuff that I got for free just for being alive and a somewhat famous person. For two years, I did some voice-over work at the Emmys. When the winners were announced, I would read arguably funny fake facts about them until they reached the stage. It was nerve-racking. I had a big metal box in front of me with a single red button, and when I pressed it, I would speak live to millions of people. I don't know why they trusted *me* to push this button, but they rewarded me for not just saying a bunch of swear words by inviting me to the gifting lounge.

The gifting lounge was a windowless room in the basement of the theater, lined with black velvet curtains and a circular buffet of swag. I could walk around the room and take whatever I wanted. There was a high-end denim station and a luxury perfume station and a station full of shiny ugly wristwatches. The hope was actual celebrities would take these products and be photographed using and wearing them. There were also weird things that no one wanted like coffee pods and hair conditioner. It was a little like a secret celebrities-only Walgreens. They assigned you a pretty young woman to carry your bag for you, which was gross. But that's where I got the one pair of jeans that I've ever looked good in, as well as a pair of bespoke Italian shoes. I had to wait to have my feet measured for the shoes because they were measuring John Lithgow's feet first. John Lithgow saw me waiting and said, "It's John Hodgman!" and I was so happy.

I still have those shoes and jeans, and I even still have my original item of swag, aka Swag Zero: the *Daily Show* holiday party gift from 2006. It was the first year I was on the show, or anything ever, for that matter. It's a black Patagonia jacket. It has the old *Daily Show with Jon Stewart* logo on the front and the old 1990s Comedy Central logo on the sleeve. Now it is frayed and worn-out. Some days I think about putting it on and going down to the new *Daily Show with Trevor Noah* to walk up and down the audience line and see if I can get people to take pictures with me, like one of those shabby, cockeyed fake Elmos in Times Square.

One night a while ago I had to walk to perform in a comedy show in Brooklyn. It was very cold out. I didn't have a proper winter jacket for some reason, so I layered up. I piled on so many sweatshirts and zippies and windbreakers that I couldn't move my arms correctly. It was ridiculous, but it felt great for some reason. It felt so great that I wore the outfit onstage, and that's when I realized *why* it felt so great: it was *all* swag. I was covered in it, encased in layer after layer of soft, protective minor fame. All those shows were over for me then, or would be soon.

Being famous is, in part, about getting things for free. (Actually: it's mostly this.) But acting, I had begun to learn, is about giving. It's about surrendering the habits and poses that protect you and becoming vulnerable: to the moment, your own emotions, and unpleasant truths. As I read the script that contained my oboe lesson and my failed seduction, I realized that I might have been invited to the beautiful party for a moment, but now that illusion was to be stripped away, along with all my clothes. And suddenly, for a reason I couldn't articulate yet, it didn't feel depressing or humiliating. It felt cleansing.

As my nude scene approached, there were a lot of conversations and paperwork. They presented me with a Nude Rider to my contract. It specified exactly what parts of my disgusting body and my shame would be revealed. "The nudity required is restricted to rear nudity," said the Nude Rider. "No genitalia, pubic hair, or anus, and no other nudity may be photographed."

Strangely, the Nude Rider was worded as though *I* had written it myself, as in: "For clarity, there will be the perception of full-frontal nudity, but I will be wearing [a] nudity belt to cover my genitalia with an oboe placed over the top." This is not a promise I had ever imagined making before, and if I were not married, it would be my go-to pickup line for the rest of my life.

We shot for two days in the Beautiful Oboist's apartment before my nude scene. The director of this episode, who was also the writer, was very kind. He took me aside for long conversations. He explained that only a few people would be on set for my scene, and if there was anyone I didn't want to be there, I should just say so. He said a person of my choosing would be standing by constantly with a thick terry-cloth robe to swoop in between takes to cover my disgusting body. He explained that everything would be arranged for my emotional comfort.

This was an alien concept to me, and especially now I wanted to say, *Why? Why do I deserve emotional comfort? I have been in the presence of actual telegenic people. I have stood in a Hollywood hotel lobby and felt the air warp behind me, some uncanny electricity that forced my body to turn and see Keira Knightley, just walking down a staircase. I had never thought much about Keira Knightley before, but when some-one's in-person beauty projects so much energy that you don't even need to see it for it to make you turn your head, to lose your breath and bearings, that's when you understand that Keira Knightley belongs on a screen, and you do not.*

I know what my face looks like now, and I know from my mirror at home what my bare body looks like, and I know that the lens will only flatten and fatten both of those things. I'm Hitler in the streets and a third-stage Guild Navigator in the sheets (look it up). So don't worry about my emotional comfort. This is going to be traumatic for everyone.

"I'll be fine," I told the director. "It will be great."

The Nude Rider specified that I would be provided a "nudity belt." The evening before my scene, I was offered a selection of Caucasian-flesh-colored privacy garments to cover my various areas. I was told no one had ever used them before, which was reassuring, as they all involved a lot of intimate nestling around and into very private curves and crevices. Some belts were more elaborate than others. One involved an array of clear rubber bands delicately linking two tan spandex panels. One was essentially just a Caucasian sock.

I tried them on in my trailer. They were all ridiculous. First, because even the "Caucasian" flesh color of these appliances was one thousand times more bronzed and healthy seeming than my bluish, skim-milky pallor. Second, they were unnecessary. "Let's not use any of these dumb underwears," I suggested to the director. "Why don't I just be naked? Why don't we invite everyone to set? Let them and the world see me as the whole nude monster that I am?"

The director said no thank you.

So on the day of my nude scene, I removed all my clothes and put on the sock. I put on my comfy robe and waited for everyone to be ready to shoot. It was the last setup of the evening, the martini shot, and it was late at night when I was told it was time. I closed Twitter and shook off my nerves and my robe. I climbed onto the young woman's bed and arranged my oboe and my smile. My smile was genuine. I was ready for my close-up. And that is how I am waiting for you, too, now. I have nothing to hide from you, because, as I said before, I can trust you.

I'm not really on television anymore. That's OK. Neither is television, really. I could tell you that in contrast to *Vacationland*, these stories are about my life and jobs in Hollywood "Workland," while I was briefly welcome in that country. But there's no hiding that these really are stories about fame, and especially its dwindling. They are stories about the many different kinds of gifting lounges, private parties, and secret societies I was given entrance to just because I was on television sometimes, and to which I am no longer invited... about New York and Los Angeles and the long, dizzying limbo I spent in the air back and forth between them before I was finally grounded, status revoked.

They are stories of unseemly ease and privilege, of course. Privilege comedy is my beat. But I recalled while waiting in the Beautiful Oboist's bed that in life, we have only our own disgusting bodies, our own strange and broken selves to offer. We have only our own stories, and it is best when you offer them nakedly. I know better now than some that when you are stripped of what hides you, whether that is fame or status or a thick terry-cloth robe like your dad used to wear, the chill on your bare skin is scary but energizing and, finally, forgiving. When you let people see you and all your junk honestly, it helps them feel seen as well.

That last part is definitely a metaphor, though. Do not get naked in front of people without their consent. I would not be the first person in comedy to expose himself without asking, so I will ask plainly: Do you want to see me in the nude? That is more of a choice than the TV show offered the Beautiful Oboist (or the viewer, for that matter).

The Beautiful Oboist had no choice but to discover me in her bedroom. I was propped up on my side in her bed, nude, happy and hopeful. Appropriately, she rejected me, and I accepted that humiliation. In many ways, it prepared me for the greatest humiliation, that of not being on television at all. Perhaps you will reject me, too. But while you decide, welcome. I will wait for you here, hidden only by my golden oboe.

Chapter Three

THANK YOU FOR
BEING GOLD

I only fly one airline, and I will refer to it here as Beloved Airlines, because I didn't want this book to be an advertisement for them. Probably that was a mistake. No one ever says they love an airline, and I bet I could have gotten some sweet sponsored content money for saying so. And anyway, you can find out what airline it is by Googling "MEDALLION STATUS." At one point, I thought about changing the title of this book to *Secret Society*, but my publisher felt that *Medallion Status* was better, and they were right, because specificity is the soul of narrative, and you deserve the specific, sick truth: I will never speak of, never mind fly, another airline, so entrenched am I in the addictive video game that is the Beloved Airlines loyalty program. Now that I think of it, maybe my publisher didn't want to change the title because they have struck their own side deal with Beloved Airlines. If so, good for them.

I fly Beloved because I have status with them. Look, they are pretty good at running an airline. They go mostly where I need to, and I like that they fly from JFK to Bangor, Maine. But it was just chance that I happened to get trapped in their particular walled garden of bonus companion tickets and slightly discounted trips and complimentary upgrades that never seem to materialize. For most of my life, I never cared which airline I took, and owed none my loyalty. Friends I knew who traveled a lot for their jobs could not understand what I was doing. One comedian friend of mine got angry at me when he learned I didn't belong to the Qantas frequent flyer program. "You're about to fly to Australia!" he said. "Do you know how many miles that is? *What are you doing, man!?*" Once I offered to fly a musician friend of mine to San Francisco so he could perform a song on a comedy show I was putting together. He asked me if I could make sure to book the ticket on Beloved Airlines. He was already deep in the game. I said sure, whatever. I asked him if he had a frequent flyer number. He recited it to me. He was very passionate about it. "It is the ankle tattoo I will never regret," he said. This dedication moved me, so I decided to sign up.

Then I had a couple of heavy travel years for comedy and book tours. I had not noticed that I had been flying Beloved Airlines more than any other. (They weren't my Beloved yet. That was when they flew under the livery of Emotionally Neutral Airways.) But one day, when I arrived at the top of the jetway for a flight to Minneapolis, the gate agent stopped me after scanning my boarding pass. She smiled and looked me in the eyes. "Thank you, Mr. Hodgman," she said. "Thank you for being Gold."

It took me a moment to process this. I guess I knew at that point that I had inadvertently racked up enough miles to qualify for Beloved Airlines Gold Medallion status. I guess I had noticed that, because of it, I got to board the plane a little earlier. But no one had ever *thanked* me for being Gold. If you are an only child who craves opportunities to follow arbitrary rules to prove that you deserve affection, then airports are already exciting places to be. But to be thanked just for *being*, and specifically for being *Gold*, activated deep, atavistic only-child pleasure centers.

No. Thank YOU, I wanted to say. *Like everyone else in the world, I always* thought *I was Gold. Or I should say, I* hoped *I was Gold. I worried a lot that I had tricked myself into* thinking *I was Gold, but secretly wasn't. I feared that the world was going to notice this someday and say, WAIT A MINUTE. HE'S NOT GOLD AT ALL! But you see me, don't you? You see my Gold!* It didn't matter that she had mispronounced my last name the way everyone does ("HAH-duh-guh-man"). She still said "Gold" perfectly, and suddenly, unexpectedly, it was the best thing to ever happen to me.

After that I started paying attention. I learned that you attain Gold by flying a certain number of miles. But these are not regular miles that you can hoard in the thousands and then redeem for, say, half a one-way flight from LaGuardia to some place no one wants to go to, or to treat yourself to a free single french fry from Seamless. These are special Medallion Qualifying Miles (MQMs). You earn them over the course of a year—and you earn more if you're flying first class. If you don't know how many MQMs you have at any moment, you can check on the Beloved Airlines website, where they have a little video game–style health bar of your progress. And you *will* check, often, because if you make Gold before the end of the year, you are guaranteed Gold for a whole *next* year. You will have locked in a whole extra year of being Gold. But if you don't hit Gold by the end of the year, you have to start over. Then you are nothing, and when you board the plane, no one will say anything to you. They won't even look at you.

(It's also possible, if you get *close* to Gold, that you actually just drop down to Silver Medallion. But that is a garbage Medallion. It is worse than nothing. It is strictly a teasing reminder of what you once held and now have lost. You are rarely thanked for being Silver, and if you are, it feels like they are making fun of you.)

I also learned that as you fly and spend more, you can go on to reach Platinum Medallion, which supposedly offers you slightly quicker access to complimentary upgrades, which I also never seem to get. Plus a gift card. And far beyond that there is Diamond Medallion, which allows you to board first and fly nude with a crossbow while sitting in the pilot's lap. This is not true, but it *is* true that Diamond Medallions receive complimentary membership in the Beloved Airlines private airport lounges. Or you can just pay money to get in. Even before I went Gold I had been in a lot of them because of a partnership Beloved Airlines has with my credit card, so I can tell you what these secret rooms are like.

The Beloved Sky Lounges (not their actual name; still not shilling) are slightly less crowded than the regular waiting areas at the boarding gates, and the chairs are slightly more stylish and comfortable, and they arc studded with power outlets. There is art on the walls and a bar offering free soda and beer and medium-shelf liquor brands. In some of the smaller Sky Lounges the bar is simply unmanned: just big bottles of vodka and whiskey that people can glug out for themselves into real-glass glasses, usually around 7 a.m.

As you know, airports occupy their own country. Let's settle this once and for all: if you have a stopover at an airport in, say, Phoenix or Berlin, you cannot say you have visited Arizona or Germany. You have only visited AIRPORT, a dimension outside the jurisdiction of not only literal local law, but also most unspoken social contracts about when it is acceptable to sleep in public, wear sweatpants, and drink and drink and drink and drink in the morning. I myself drink a free drink whenever possible, but to my own surprise, I have never succumbed to this morning temptation. Perhaps I fear emitting the same giddy light that I see in the faces of all the other middle-aged moms and dads when they sip their first vodka-sodas and breakfast Sam Adamses in the Sky Lounge, the smiles and shining eyes that say:

Finally. I am alive again. For the first time since college, or maybe high school, I am freed from the drudgery of work and childcare and decent behavior that I use to distract myself from the grim drift of my body, my enflabbening into the picture of my own mom or dad. Suddenly I am not afraid of dying on this flight to Atlanta. Or ever. In fact, part of me hopes the plane does *go down, because it will never, ever get better than this.*

Once in a Sky Lounge, I noticed the self-serve bar had a bottle of Fernet-Branca, an esoteric Italian digestif that tastes like pine cones soaked in menthol and grave dirt that is favored by hipster chefs and weirdo booze completists like me who used to write about non-wine alcohol for magazines. I pitied the poor cocktail nerd who put it there. The Sky Lounge bar is no place for mixology. The Sky Lounge is not aspirational. It is desperational.

But the food is pretty good! There is usually a spread of bagels and crackers and hummus and other happy ballast. There are spicy snack mixes that you empty out of tall Lucite silos into little ramekins. There are broccoli florets and cherry tomatoes and shards of celery the temperature of the Arctic. There are tuna salads and chicken salads, which are dangerous and mayonnaise-y enough to leave lying around *without* their being fondled and breathed on by countless travelers and their global biome of bacteria and secretions. Still, I eat it all. Swine flu scares me, but there is a tray of cubed pepper Jack cheese that *never runs out*, and next to it is ranch dressing, and it is all for me.

There is also some truly-more-than-pretty-good food. I am always amazed that the Sky Lounge is able to pump out so many hard-boiled eggs that consistently do *not* have a green ring around the yolk. So many actual restaurants fail in this regard. I cannot help but take a picture of those beautiful chalky yellow yolks, and that is why my Instagram account is so unappealing.

I have discovered that the best jambalaya in the city of New Orleans comes out of the electric crock in the Sky Lounge in Louis Armstrong International Airport. This statement is not controversial, because it is true. Any soup or stew deepens in flavor the longer it simmers at a very low temperature, cools, reheats, and simmers again. And up in the Sky Lounge, this cycle happens for days. (This is not slander but hyperbole, Beloved Airlines. Legal hyperbole. Keep your Beloved Lawyers away from me.)

For a while the Sky Lounge offered a Thai-style chicken-and-rice soup. They called it "Wicked" Thai Chicken and Rice Soup, which is offensive in the context of the history of demonization of Asia by the West, but accurate in the context of how the bullies I knew in Boston talked, because it was goddamned delicious. Then they took it away, suddenly, and the Sky Lounge became my enemy. It was an uncomfortable time.

But eventually the Sky Lounge sensed my anger and started offering pho. This earned not only my forgiveness but my respect. I appreciate that pho is everywhere now and all of America is drenched in Sriracha. But please remember that I am elderly and recall a time when Vietnamese noodle soup was still esoteric and knowing where the best pho shop in Seattle was was the height of food snob cred on the Chowhound message boards.

But now the Sky Lounge was (and is still!) offering great

urns of ginger-fragrant pho broth for you to customize with rice noodles, tofu, cilantro, and scallions, all sitting out in sneeze-guarded little bowls. No beef tendon, but still: respect. It is, in fact, wicked good. And more credit to Sky Lounge, they do not call it "Wicked" or "Crafty" or "Inscrutable Asian Soup." They call it Sky Broth, which is problematic in its erasure of its history and origin, yes, but I say again: it is called Sky Broth. In this case, I am *not* changing the name, because it is one of the strangest and dumbest combination of words that I have ever encountered, and I love it.

Some of the Sky Lounges also have a patio where, in warmer months, travelers who have always wished to stand on the roof of an airport terminal and smell jet fuel can finally do so. They have scattered the deck with ottomans and chaise longues, and you can sit out there with your Diet Coke, and in between engine roars, you can hear the gentle *bump-hiss* of chill-out club music.

The Sky Lounges used to be hidden behind barely marked doors like secret societies. They were for high-level initiates only. But now that airlines understand that they are profit centers, this is no longer true. They are easy to find. Just look for the signs that lead you to the sliding doors that open upon an aspirin-white parlor full of older businessmen who are SO ANGRY that their particular boarding zone does not allow them free access to the lounge. These guys are always there, fuming. Even though I have that deal with my credit card, I would still pay a lot to get to walk past these mad business dads on my way into the Sky Lounge. How much? Roughly all of my money. That may seem like bad math to a business dad. But I was a liberal arts major who never managed to balance my checkbook: I was never supposed to have status over these guys.

The first time I flew first class was when I was twenty-one. I was flying to Buenos Aires, ostensibly to do research on the author Jorge Luis Borges. If that sounds pretentious, it's because I was. I was also a newly minted con artist, having scammed $1,000 off the Yale Spanish Department to underwrite my trip, money that had been earmarked for actual Latin American Studies students who wanted to do more than stroll around a beautiful fake Paris, visiting a few of the places where their favorite authors had worked, but otherwise staying up all night with other Americans, eating steaks and smoking and buying European comic books at the all-night newsstands at four in the morning. But too bad for those Latin American Studies students, because I decided I wanted their money and I took it.

I booked my flight on United. Sorry, Beloved. I was younger then, and also United played "Rhapsody in Blue" on their television ads, and I had that Gershwin cassette on *heavy* rotation in my bathroom boom box. I listened to that big clarinet glissando that opens "Rhapsody in Blue" every morning before school. I was a clarinetist myself, after all, and also an incredibly cool person.

The night flight from Miami had been delayed several hours. A lot of passengers had given up and made other arrangements, so as we boarded, the plane was almost empty. People were opening blankets and laying across whole rows of economy seats, and I could have done the same. But as I found my crummy seat, I realized I had just walked through a completely empty first class cabin. I was curious, privileged, dumb, and emboldened by my recent heist of Spanish Department funds. I turned around. It was time to see what this cool, Gershwin-loving dude was capable of.

I approached the first class flight attendant standing by the flimsy curtain that separated our worlds. "Excuse me," I said. "Can I sit in there?"

She did not say yes. But to my surprise, she did not say no.

"I'm sorry," she said, "I actually don't think I can let you, because I don't think we have an extra first class meal to serve you."

I told her I didn't care about the *meal*. Not at *all*. I just wanted to sit in the nice seat.

But as I explained this, I was confused. The first class flight attendant didn't need to give me a *reason* for saying no. Even then I understood I was not entitled to a reason. Or more accurately, saying no *was* the reason, the *whole* reason this flimsy curtain was here. People don't pay for first class to get nicer seats and legroom and ramekins of warm nuts. Those are the perks (except for the nuts, which are gross). The service they are paying for is to be in a place where others cannot be. What's more, status doesn't count unless other people *see* you having it. That is why the coach passengers are boarded last and marched past the first class passengers as they are receiving their preflight drinks. That is why, even when the curtain is drawn, you can see right through it. That is why when a white, able-bodied twenty-one-year-old man asks, "Can I sit in there," you tell him *no*, loudly. You don't go back and rummage around until you find an extra first class meal for him, and then apologetically offer him a nice seat and warm nuts.

But that is what she did.

I sat down. A man ushered a whiskey into my hand. It was in an actual glass. I drank it. I felt my brain change shape the way everyone's does when they first sit in first class. First there is disbelief and euphoria. You touch all the little seat-adjustment buttons and the sleeping masks and cozy socks and want to cry. You feel so lucky. Then they bring the meal for you, the one they found for you, the one that probably the flight attendant was going to eat herself. It is served on a real plate with real flatware and cloth napkins, and as you fall asleep, you will think to yourself, *You know, it's a good thing she* did *find that extra meal for me. It would have been bullshit if she hadn't. She's lucky I don't complain.*

When you get away with something brash and ridiculous and unfair, it is natural for you to feel that it is perfectly natural. You comfort yourself with free whiskey and say it is right that this whiskey is free, that the nuts are warm, and it's not at all unfair, because those unhumans behind me weren't smart or talented or hardworking enough to take advantage of a flight attendant who obviously had eaten a bunch of drugs or something. Like all status, if you get into first class, you have to believe you deserve it. And for that reason, once you leave a first class cabin, you feel robbed, wronged, and unnatural, and so you spend your life anxiously, *always* trying to get back in.

Later that year, I was flying with my mom and dad from Boston to some other city. There was a delay, and I said this was great news. I told my dad: Now is your chance. Go tell them that we all want to sit in first class now. It works. They do this all the time! He didn't do it. And I am ashamed to recall that I thought in that moment that my dad's decision was not based on experience, decency, and non-assholism, but cowardice. I'm sorry, Dad.

But that was long ago. Now I was Gold, and everyone was thanking me for it. And not long after I went Gold, I was offered a spot in the cast of a television show that was shooting in Los Angeles. I knew it would mean a lot of travel and being apart from my wife and our children. It didn't pay a lot. But the production would pay for my flights to and from Los Angeles, and they would be contractually obliged to fly me first class, back and forth across the country, over and over. I knew I would log a lot of Sky Lounge time. I knew I would rack up a lot of MQMs.

"Would they fly me on Beloved Airlines?" I asked my agent.

"Sure, I guess," my agent said.

I took the job. And very quickly, I went Platinum.

"Thank you for being Platinum" does not sound as good as "Thank you for being Gold." But I had drunk the Sky Broth, and I was not going back.

Chapter Four

SECRET FAMILY

Most of my previous acting roles had been limited, and they didn't last long. Usually either my character was killed, or the show would be canceled. I would warn showrunners of this trend early on after they hired me. *Kill me quick*, I would tell them. *Either my character dies, or the show does.*

The exception, for a while, was this new job in Los Angeles. It was a comedy about a married couple who were having trouble adjusting to middle age. They had wacky best friends, and I played the third best friend of the male lead. The first and second best friends were a man and a woman, both much better actors than I was. They played college pals of Leading Best Friend. My character was initially Leading Best Friend's accountant, and then his employer, and then his employee. I suppose he needed me in his life in case something happened to the other friends, like the president pro tempore of the Senate of Best Friendship.

Sometimes I would forget I was on this television show. It

shot only a few months a year, and I was not on it very much. I would be biding my time at home when suddenly a call would come in, and I would remember: *Oh, right. I'm still on TV.* On the other end of the call, a voice would tell me I was needed for a scene in which I had to encourage my Leading Best Friend to hire a prostitute, or to harass my coworkers by walking around the office with fake gray pubic hair hanging out of my pants. (I was your basic John Hodgman–type character.) Then I would fly out for two nights, come home for three days, and then back out for four nights, and so on. At least once I flew overnight to LA, picked up my rental car, drove to the office space where we were shooting, immediately got into wardrobe, said my words and made my faces (this is called acting), drove back to the airport, and flew home again.

The television show offered a modest lodging stipend, and at first I stayed in a hotel. The Hotel was a very fancy and historic Hollywood hotel that looks like a French castle. The stipend did not even come close to covering the cost of the Hotel, but I had stayed there during fancier times in my career and I loved it. The first time I ever walked into the lobby, before I even checked in, the woman at the host stand said my favorite words: "It's John Hodgman!" Later I would ask the manager of the Hotel if the woman at the host stand had been coached to say those words. He said no. He thought she was just a fan. This was a lie that I accepted for many years. And through this bond, the manager of the Hotel and I gradually became friends. His name is Phil.

My family was with me on that first trip, but not this time. The morning before I began work on the first episode of the television show, I left my wife and children at the breakfast table in Maine. They were smiling but sad to see me go, and bathed in cool Maine summer sunshine. I entered a long, gross hallway of cars and airports and planes and airports and cars, and by evening I was sitting in the wobbly yellow candlelight on the Hotel patio, eating dinner at a table for one. Jessica Lange was at the next table. Jessica Lange, of course, is most famous for being my imaginary girlfriend whom I met while watching the movie *Tootsie*. Now Jessica Lange was telling her dinner partner that with her *and* Kathy Bates on the show this season, it should really be called *American Horror Story: Menopause*. I texted this to all my friends. The Hotel is very secretive, and it frowns on people reporting what happens there, but I feel Jessica Lange deserves that the world know: she is very funny.

The next day I went in to work on the television show. We mostly shot on location in actual homes and restaurants and karaoke bars in the San Fernando Valley. I always stopped for breakfast at the craft services table before I did my acting. There is little I like more than a steam tray full of breakfast sausages—ask anyone—and craft services is very good on this account.

On my first day of work, I had to drive a car into a strip mall parking lot to meet my Leading Best Friend. They showed me the very small piece of tape on the ground where I had to stop the car in order to be framed correctly in camera. I hit my mark perfectly almost every take. The camera man complimented me, and it is hard to overstate how proud I was.

It all went so smoothly that I had completed my work for the day and was back at the Hotel by mid-afternoon. I sat by the pool and watched a bunch of wealthy, idle Europeans suck the sun into their weirdly shaped and wholly bared bodies. They did not care about their pouches and curves and ripples and folds and moles and hairs. I was in the shade and wondered what it would be like to feel that way. Near me, a young woman in a bathing suit was drinking champagne with two suitors. She had a number of tattoos on her legs and one of her suitors asked what a certain tattoo meant, and she couldn't remember. They laughed and laughed. Then I went up to my room for a nap. It was an incredible afternoon. Wasn't this worth leaving my family for?

But it turns out, making the television show was not all fun and breakfast sausages and poolside naps and forgotten tattoos. Because it turns out that as good as my car acting was, my regular acting was not so good. I learned this the next time I went in to work. It was a new episode. I was driven to a new location in the Valley, a print shop where my character was a manager, and I met this episode's director. I liked her very much, but once I started saying my words and making my faces, she kept stopping me.

"Stop making those faces," she would say. She told me that

I was mugging. She needed me to stop making the jokes sound like jokes. She needed me to be natural.

"Be smaller," she told me.

I didn't know what to say. Actually, that's not true. I knew what I *had* to say was "Got it. Thank you," and so I did. The truth was, I didn't know what to *do*.

This was outside of my experience in two ways. First, what passed for my acting on *The Daily Show* and elsewhere had always been about landing jokes in the biggest, fakest way possible (this is apart from my car acting, though, which everyone agrees is powerful and subtle). Second, I had long ago learned that when you are shooting a television show, time is more important than any one performance. If you are doing a bad job at acting, I had learned, they will not bother to tell you. That would be a waste of time, and it might put you into an emotional hole that would also waste time. And by the same token, I had learned that when they say you have done a *good* job at acting, they are probably lying.

But now here was the Director, breaking that rule. I felt bad and also bad for her. She didn't have the time to take me aside and discreetly give me years of training and experience in acting. So she ended up having to trick me. She gave me chores to do in my fake office. Folders to pick up and forms to sign and papers to drop off as I walked my circuit, talking over my shoulder to my Leading Best Friend. All so I would not turn the jokes into jokes. So that I would seem like a natural human being, as if that had ever been an option for me.

"Be smaller," she would still say. "Smaller, smaller."

Later that season, the Director and I worked together again at an old three-story mansion in Jefferson Park. The house was pillared and decayed and used frequently as a setting for scary movies. Wandering it between takes I found a pentagram painted in blood red on the floor in the basement, and a second-floor bedroom that was empty except for dozens of creepy dolls, scattered on the floor. Why hadn't anyone cleaned up the dolls after the last shoot? Or were the dolls permanent, just held here in reserve should a future movie need a creepy doll scene? Maybe it was a selling point. Or maybe I was the only one who could see the dolls. I spent a lot of time up in that room contemplating this mystery. (Check my Instagram.)

The house was not portraying a haunted house in our show, however. It was doubling as a frat house, which to me was scarier. In the scene we were shooting, my Leading Best Friend and I had to go to this house and demand money that is owed to us by a particular frat bro named Doogie. But Doogie's frat bros tell us he's not home, so we leave. As we walk down the stairs from the house, my character decides to fix the situation by tweeting angrily at Doogie, which is always effective.

"Stop," the Director said immediately as I began my tweeting. "John, stop." She said my tweeting looked fake. She was right. I was just typing random nonsense into my phone. She could tell from twenty feet away.

"Write actual words," she said. And I did, and it was much

better. If you want to see what I wrote, just search my Twitter account for the words: "Doogie please resoind to my emai."

A small part of what made acting hard for me was that it was not clear why Leading Best Friend and I would be friends in the first place. Both the actor and the character are tall, handsome, athletic, affable, and liked. And I was me, the stunted weirdo deformed brother who never comes downstairs but instead only hangs out in his furnitureless room taking pictures of his creepy dolls.

In real life, Leading Best Friend was also from Massachusetts, which gave us a little bit to talk about. But he had grown up in a different town playing hockey, a sport he continued to play and enjoyed watching. My efforts to engage him on *my* favorite sport—the history of logos of extinct hockey teams—only went so far.

At some point I did come down from my room full of dolls. Feeling low and bad about my acting, I sat at the bottom of the stairs playing Scrabble against the computer on my phone. This was back when I was playing Scrabble a lot. I was pretty good at it. You probably remember from all the games my wife and I played as I live-tweeted the results: I knew how to drop seven-tile bingos for fifty extra points, I knew all the non-U uses of Q, and I was pretty deft at hitting those double- and triple-letter-score spaces.

My Leading Best Friend took interest in my game.

"Do you play?" I asked.

He said yes. He said he often played Words with Friends. I told him there is no Words with Friends in this life: there is only Scrabble, with enemies. He laughed at that and suggested we play. It was a nice gesture on his part, and also I thought it would make me feel better to flatten this dumb handsome hockey player beneath the weight of all my sweet bingos.

That is not how it happened, however. I had a strongish early game, but it was only his third or fourth turn when he packed an H and M against SMALL to form SH, HM, and MM, hitting the triple-word square with H twice for a total of something like six thousand points. I realized that Hockey Man knew his two-letter words cold. I had no chance. Over the next few moves he casually dropped BOOSTS, BOLSTERS, SULFURS, and XU on my head before finally emptying his rack with KREWE and handing me my phone back.

"Good game," he said.

Smaller, smaller.

But no matter what happened at work, at the Hotel, I never felt small. That was the danger of it. I would return from a day of shooting and the graceful woman at the bottom of the driveway, the one whose job it was to coldly turn unwanted people away, would instead smile at me and say, "Welcome home."

Justin at the little bar in the lobby would know I wanted a martini and make it without asking and talk to me about the Hartford Whalers or some other extinct hockey team I was obsessed with. And there I was: sitting at a bar, talking to a man about sports (or as close as I was ever going to get to talking about sports). I would feel a sudden sense of normalness, of welcome in the culture, and I knew it was false, but I accepted that gift. This generosity was only exceeded by the time I put out a call on Twitter to ask if anyone in LA knew where to find scrapple. If you do not know what scrapple is, the name really says it all: it is mushy gray cake of cornmeal, sage, and leftover pig hearts, livers, tongues, and skin. In Philadelphia and Baltimore and some other places, you cut it into crumbly slices and fry it and then you eat it on purpose, because it is delicious and hilariously honest. It does not hide what it is. The only more truth in advertising it could offer were if it weren't called scrapple but "Genuine Gray Offal-Loaf."

I wanted the scrapple for a joke I wanted to play on a late-night television show I was going to tape. But I despaired of getting it. You almost never saw it in stores outside the mid-Atlantic. I don't know how long it was after I tweeted—one hour? not more than two—when there was a knock on my hotel room door. A room service waiter offered me a tray and on the tray sat a pound of scrapple, defrosted, compliments of the house. This is still the greatest magic trick I've ever seen. I didn't end up making the joke on television. I blew it off so I could fry up slices of scrapple on my hotel suite's little art deco stove and eat it, by myself.

It is hard to feel lonely at the Hotel, even when you are alone in your room eating scrapple. You can go down to the big lobby in the afternoon and see this or that most famous person in the world sitting right across from you, also alone, and it feels like you are all just loafing around in the living room of your family house together, and you and Charlize Theron over there, reading a book, are secret siblings. Often I would get a room whose window faced the patio, so at night, alone in bed, I could fall asleep to the clatter and murmur of the late diners below. It was comforting, like falling asleep to a downstairs dinner party hosted by my and Charlize's sophisticated mom and handsome stepdad.

If you *really* want to be alone at the Hotel, you have to go to the gym. No one wants to go to the gym at this Hotel, and even the Hotel hates the concept of fitness, with its air of virtue and discipline. That is why the "gym" is just one treadmill and one elliptical machine and a photogenic but unused heavy bag all shoved into what is essentially an attic crawlspace. No one ever goes there. I take it back. One time I went to the gym and Ralph Fiennes was there doing curls with some silver dumbbells and listening to the Rolling Stones very loudly.

"I'm sorry," Ralph Fiennes said. "Is the music too loud?"

"No," I said. "This is all totally perfect."

(I double-take it back. Sometimes you might see Tom Sizemore in the gym, doing manic bicep curls while still fully dressed in street clothes. Truth be told, it's sometimes a mixed bag in the celeb department at the Hotel. The point is, the Hotel is full of weird serendipities and bright distractions, and you never feel small.)

On one night after shooting the television show, all of the following things happened: I got back and the Graceful Woman in the driveway said, "Welcome home." I went to the patio to have dinner alone. It was a beautiful early evening, and I was looking forward to a quiet night and an early bedtime. But then I got a text from a friend. He said he had just left our mutual friend, a screenwriter, in his room at the Hotel, and now the Screenwriter wanted me to come up. My friend said the Screenwriter had a surprise for me. So I went up. The Screenwriter greeted me at the door saying I was about to be surprised, and then he let me in. There were two women in his room, friends of his from Denmark, and they were hiding. They weren't doing a good job, however. One was hiding behind a very slender potted plant. The other was hiding under a glass coffee table. When I came into the room, they said, "Surprise!" Then they left.

Then the Screenwriter took me down to dinner and sat me between a famous director and an actor from the television show *Lost*, and also all of a sudden Benedict Cumberbatch was there, at the table next to us, with a large group of friends. Someone slid me a drink because we are all famous friends together, and then all of a sudden Benedict Cumberbatch was alone, under the table with his phone light on, looking for his dropped credit card. He found it, and then came back up and apologized to me.

"I'm sorry," said Benedict Cumberbatch, and then, even though it was loud and I couldn't quite hear him, I swear he said, "My mother just died."

Which I now know from Wikipedia was not true and still isn't, but I am sure he said it. Or at least I cannot figure out what else Benedict Cumberbatch was trying to convey to me before I was spotted and then hugged by Griffin Dunne, and after a long, deep conversation with him, I went to rejoin my acquaintance, who had gone to another table. There I was seated next to a different young Danish woman named Reggae who complimented me on my mustache.

"Your mustache is tight," she said. "It reminds me of my dad's mustache."

"Good night," I said.

The Screenwriter intercepted me before I got to the elevator. He was angry. "Where are you going?" he said. "She said your mustache is tight!" I tried to explain to him that, while I enjoy implausible adventures and the brief, vertiginous feeling of wondering if Benedict Cumberbatch is playing mind games with me, the fact is, there is no one I want to hug and kiss other than my wife. This luminous night was now growing shadowed by the desperate and the transgressive, and I could only see it getting darker from here. And anyway, the illusion that any of this was meant for *me* was broken the moment Reggae complimented my mustache. I know what my mustache looks like. I know that no one wants it, not even a Danish person. This was a castle of lies.

My acquaintance did not accept this. "I think you are an elitist," he said.

After this I stopped staying at the Hotel for a while. I was starting to feel it was not a healthy place for me, and I also realized that if I were going to be leaving my family behind to work here, I might as well try to actually keep some of the modest money I was making, rather than throwing all my earnings at the Hotel as quickly and as hard as possible.

After this, I began staying with my friends Paul F. Tompkins and Janie Haddad. Paul is a brilliant comedian, and if you like comedy, you know exactly who he is. If you don't know Janie, you should, because she is a wonderful, funny actor and human being who also happens to be married to Paul. They had just bought their first home, an adorable house on the final adorable block of an adorable residential neighborhood bordering the vaguely damp concrete trench called the Los Angeles River. It was the perfect size for a childless couple. It was slightly less than the perfect size for a previously childless couple who are forced to take in their deadbeat adult son (that's me). They should not have, but nevertheless did give me their guest bedroom over and over as I was flown back and forth across the country. Sometimes I would stay with them for weeks.

We always had a nice time together. If I was not working during the day, Janie and I would gossip or walk around the neighborhood. We would make plans for dinner, and when Paul got home, we would make that dinner and eat it on our laps in front of the television, just like I used to do in high school with my mom and dad. Once I had to fly from Los Angeles to Boston to perform in a comedy festival. Paul and Janie happened to be there as well, so we spent the afternoon walking up and down Newbury Street and had dinner together at a French restaurant. I was near where I grew up, within three hundred miles of my wife and children for the first time in weeks. But I did not manage to see them. I had to fly from Boston right back to LA the next day. In fact, Paul and Janie did too, and we were on the same flight, so I could drive them in my rental car back to the home we shared. Once we got in, I made myself a martini in the monogrammed cocktail shaker Paul had gotten me as a gift, and we watched television. Our little family trip had come to a close.

One evening in LA, Janie was making dinner. Paul was watching the news while ironing some shirts in the living room. I was in my own room, just hanging out with my computer. I realized that I was doing exactly what I presume my teenage daughter does when *she* hides out in her room before dinner: talking to middle-aged men on the internet.

Unlike my daughter, however, my bedroom door was *open*. It wasn't a *rule* or anything. I just loved my fake mom and dad and had nothing to hide from them.

"John, do you want any shirts ironed?" Paul called to me.

"No thanks, Dad!" I said.

Then Janie called out to say that dinner would be ready by 7 p.m., and I calmly called back to say, "JESUS, MOM! I KNOW ALREADY! I HAVE A CLOCK, YOU KNOW! I WILL BE OUT AT SEVEN. WHY DON'T YOU GUYS TRUST ME?"

But sometimes Paul and Janie would go away for a few nights without me. You would think that with them gone, I would throw a huge house party and dance in my underwear to old rock songs, but that did not happen. Once I was alone, I could not ignore that where once I had been living the big-spender life at the Hotel, now I was saving pennies in a borrowed back bedroom of an empty house. I was in a new neighborhood and I had to figure out where to sign up for a gym membership and which was the good grocery store. When my hosts were away, I would shop for myself and eat solo dinners in front of the same third episode of *Daredevil* on Netflix before falling asleep on the couch, over and over. I thought I had been reliving my youth as a cared-for only child, but without Paul and Janie there, I realized now I was more a like a sad, divorced dad.

One time Paul and Janie went to a weekend wedding to which I was not invited. (Thanks a LOT, Mark and Kristina. But I still love you.) That Friday I worked at the television show and came back late to an empty house. It had been a long day of faces and words, and I was tired. I don't know how it happened, but this time, after I fell asleep in front of the third episode of *Daredevil* on Netflix again, I did *not* wake up on the couch at 3 a.m. as Netflix was once again rolling into the credits on the season finale. This time, I woke up in Paul and Janie's bed. I was under the covers, and I was cuddling a clutch of plastic clothes hangers. I don't know where I found them. I guess I was lonely.

The light in the window was predawn, pale blue. I got up, straightened their bed, and went back to my own room. When I woke up, it was midmorning. I went back into their bedroom to stare at the bed and ponder my moral obligations. Paul and Janie would not be back for a few days, and I would be gone by then, back to New York. I didn't want to tell them what had happened, and probably didn't have to. The bed looked pretty neat and clean. For all I knew, I had only spent ten minutes in there. But there was the problem of the hangers. My theory was that they had been left on the bed after Paul or Janie had finished packing, and I had found them there as I sleepwalked in and mistook them for a wife or a blankie.

I stand by that detective work, especially since the alternative explanation was that before getting into their bed, I first pawed through their closets for hurty things to sleep with. That doesn't make any sense. If I had opened their closets, why wouldn't I have taken one of Paul's beautiful suits that I coveted? That would have been pathologically disturbing, but it would at least have some narrative heft.

I decided to put the hangers back on the bed where I had probably found them. I experimented with different scatter patterns, but it was pointless. There was no way to remember how they were arranged, and Paul and Janie were sure to spot the difference. Maybe they had even left them there as a trap, the way James Bond taught you to lay a hair across your doorway to see if anyone was sneaking into your room while you were out. (PS: No one was ever sneaking into your room. No one ever cared.)

I knew I had to come clean and tell them what happened. But wouldn't this necessitate washing the bedding and remaking the bed? Of course it would. And wouldn't they take that as a tacit admission that I had wet their bed? Well, probably not.

They probably would just presume I had *shat* their bed. As anyone would presume.

I began to appreciate that the only acceptable solution was for me to burn the sheets, fill the entire house with Purell, and then leave the earth. But I decided to postpone this plan. I had received an invitation to have dinner at the Hotel. The invitation came from essentially strangers—friends of a friend of a friend. Having dinner with them was in no way convenient to me or, frankly, desired. But I wanted to put this all behind me, and I wanted to see the Hotel again. The Hotel was the sort of place where if you soiled the bed, no one would judge you. It would be part of some wild adventure and not some weird shame puzzle that I had to solve.

I took an Uber to the Hotel and got dropped off at the bottom of the driveway. I didn't see the Graceful Woman who normally greeted me. I thought it might be her night off. Instead there was a cadre of young handsome men in matching peacoats. They were surprised to see me.

"Where have you been?" they asked. "Why aren't you staying with us?"

"Oh, I'm sorry, fake friends," I said. "I have been staying with *actual* friends. I know, I know, I agree with you: it's disgusting. But I'm embarrassed to admit that I have been trying to save money, and in truth my real friends have been very kind and good company. And I have repaid them by sleeping and sweating and maybe doing other things in their bed, and I am afraid to look."

I didn't say this, of course. Sometimes I take some license in my retellings, but I promise I will always let you know, and I promise you that the rest of this actually *did* happen. I *did* actually say, "I'm sorry, I'm staying with friends." And then I did actually see the Graceful Woman. She emerged from some hidden corner, back from her break, I guess. This time she did not say, "Welcome home." This time she leveled me with her eyes and said, "Judas Iscariot." She spoke it into the unlikely but appropriate chill of an early Los Angeles spring: a joke that was not exactly a joke.

Ha ha, I laughed. I apologized again for not spending all my money here, and I meant it, and she seemed to forgive me. "How have you been?" I asked, as though I were talking to a fond family member after a long absence.

"Oh, fine!" she said. She looked past me as she spoke. "I've spent the past fifteen years of my life standing at the bottom of this driveway, and I have nothing to show for it," she said. "How could I be better?"

I didn't know what to say or how to account for this sudden knifelike candor that cut us both, somehow. Was she confiding in me? Was it because I had earned her trust at some point that I had not noticed? Or was it because I was nothing to her? As I was no longer a regular at the Hotel, she might as well have been talking to a shadow on the wall. Or maybe she was punishing me, and everyone, for believing in the castle of lies in the first place.

"I'm sorry," I said.

But then a young, famous couple arrived. She smiled and kissed them on their cheeks. "Have fun, kids," she said. I went in after them. Dinner was fine.

When I got back to my little fake home there was no one to greet me. I did wash the sheets, of course. As far as I could tell, I had not fouled them in any way, and I felt lucky.

Before I left, I wrote a note explaining what had happened with the bed and the hangers. I propped it up on a set of cocktail trays I had got them as a gift. You might say, *Trays? That is a terrible gift.* But they were nice, modern, geometric nesting trays. They were nice enough I felt I had to write on the card, "Please know I bought these for you a long time ago. They are meant to say *thank you.* Not *I am sorry I shat your bed*, which is a thing that DID NOT HAPPEN."

I think they believed me. They still use the trays, and I still stay with them from time to time. Home is where they have to take you in. I just made up that line because I am a famous poet.

Chapter Five

RACKING UP MILES

During this time I was also racking up MQMs as I flew around the country performing my imitation of stand-up comedy. I never felt comfortable calling myself a stand-up comic, and I don't think stand-up comics liked me calling myself that either, so I stopped. Stand-up, like acting, is a very special performance skill that I also never trained for. And also, a stand-up's job is to be funny no matter what. I can tell funny stories onstage, but sometimes I don't want to be funny, and sometimes I'm just not. I never could find a big closing joke to blow away the house at the end of my act. But dressing up as Ayn Rand and singing "We're in the Money" with a ukulele covers a lot of sins. I guess technically that makes me a prop comic. In any case, sometimes people bought tickets to see me do this, and so I would fly out to meet them.

Once I spent a week in Portland, Oregon. Portland is a nice city. Right from the moment you get there, you see how nice it is. The Portland airport is clean and small and manageable.

There is a piano in the middle of Concourse D that anyone is welcome to play. When I arrived, it was late at night. A young man in a custodian uniform sat down at the piano and just suddenly started playing beautiful classical music. I don't know what piece, because I am not a custodian in Portland, but that's the kind of city it is: one that values art and civic virtue and the hidden talents of its citizens.

The people of Portland are nice. They all ride bicycles and scooters and make hand signals before they turn. If you go to a rock show, people at the show will not just go to the bar to get a beer. They will form a line, perpendicular to the bar, with great vacant stretches of bar on either side. They wait their turn, one after the other. And the rock show doesn't happen in an empty crowded basement shoved full of people who are likely to die in a fire. Instead, the rock club looks like a ski lodge, like the Overlook Hotel, with vast woolen carpets, leather banquettes, and a roaring fireplace. And when the show starts, when people in other cities will stand up and move closer to the stage to see the act, a person in Portland will sit down, on a quilted ottoman, with a hot toddy, and that person will get angry at anyone who is not sitting down in the rock club, which is to say everyone else, and that person will grab your jacket, or I should say, my jacket, and tug on it. And then when you turn around, she will literally hiss at you and say, "I can't fucking see." So you see, it's not merely that the people in Portland are nice: they are nicer than you and everyone else in the world, and so they deserve clear fucking sightlines, and you don't.

If this happens, do what I did. Just say, "Excuse me. If you would like my attention, just tap me on the shoulder and say, 'Excuse me.' Don't tug on my jacket. Treat me like I am also a human being. After all, I am from Park Slope, so I also deserve whatever I want at all times."

I don't know why I make fun of Portland. Every joke about Portland is a cliché at this point. And if you want clichés about Portland, Portland is more than happy to offer them for you.

And the truth is, I had a lovely time there. I did a lovely show. And the audience was great. I made sure everyone could see me. After the show I was amazed to see my old friend Patrick in the audience. Patrick and I had once worked together at a video store when I was in college. I had not seen him since then, and only the week before had mentioned onstage that I missed him. And now here he was. Patrick and I caught up. We talked about the video store and the time the very famous actor came in looking for adult movies. I will tell you about that later. Patrick makes beer and cider and polishes geodes. Portland is a good place for him.

When I left the next night, I passed that piano again, which really is lovely, and this time, an older man in his seventies was playing some other kind of classical music, as an older woman who I presume was his wife or girlfriend listened. It was the second most magical thing I saw in Portland after the conjuring of Patrick.

After Portland I went to Philadelphia. Philadelphia is called "The City of Brotherly Love," which is a lie. Philadelphia is not a nice city. I am allowed to say this because my mother was from there, and I love the city, and I think it feels OK about me. But you can't be sure. Even Philadelphians will tell you that there is a lot of angry energy there. Even the young oddballs who like my imitation of stand-up comedy get ruinously drunk at my shows and often have to be asked to leave. It's one of the only places I've been openly heckled, and that guy was wearing a *Doctor Who* scarf.

Sometimes when you do a show in a city, they will send a car to your hotel for you. I used to like to stay at the Radisson because it was across the street from a twenty-four-hour diner called Little Pete's. When I arrived this time, I only had a short while before the car was supposed to pick me up, so I threw my bags on the bed and ran across to Little Pete's to eat scrapple and eggs as quickly as possible.

Then my driver came. Philadelphia, like Boston, is the sort of city where if you get into a cab or a hired town car and the driver is a white person, he will presume that you are also racist. As my driver steered me to my show at Temple University, he kept trying to let me know, in coded language, that this was a very different part of town. He would say subtle things like, "You have to be careful in this part of town," and "It's so dirty here. Why don't they take care of their own neighborhood?" and "Look at all that trash," and "The people who live here are not as good as white people."

Well. Not that last one.

"Do you get what I'm trying to say?" he asked.

I got it. It never occurred to him that I might be offended. Maybe because I look like Hitler, or maybe because I just stared straight ahead and said nothing.

The students at Temple were amazing. It was probably the most racially mixed crowd I had ever performed for. I worried that my brand of esoteric-privilege comedy, honed for a decade in front of countless audiences of white people in their thirties and forties, might not work in this room. So I did some advance pandering research. I learned that the sports teams at Temple are called the Owls. Their rivals, I also learned, are the Penn State Nittany Lions. I said that I hoped the Owls would devour the Nittany Lions, and then regurgitate them in a compact little bolus of pelt and bones, and they enjoyed that, proving once again that owl biology jokes cross all class and race divides. The students also enjoyed my impersonation of Ayn Rand, but maybe more because I had to get naked in front of them to change into my Ayn Rand dress. Anyway, the show was great and it reminded me: racist cabdrivers are wrong, and you know that even when you're in the cab and you can say something about it. Or you can just get out of the car and walk the rest of the way. That neighborhood is fine.

After the show I went to a bar called Dirty Frank's to meet a bunch of listeners of my podcast. I had just recorded an episode in Portland two days before with a young couple named Drew and Lindy, and now they were here in this very bar. Philadelphia conjured them for me. Drew showed me his Philadelphia Flyers tattoo and I talked about extinct hockey with him.

At the bar, no one lined up, and the bartender took her time no matter how much you tipped her, and a young guy accepted a beer I bought him and said, "So what's it like to be famous, George?" His girlfriend reminded him that my name was John, and he said, "Great. I fucked up the famous guy's name."

And then I went to Little Pete's by myself at 2 a.m. and ate my second helping of scrapple in five hours. No one talked to me and no one played piano, and I thought this is a nice city. And even though Little Pete's is closed now, I still think that's true.

Here are some other nice cities I visited when I was flying all over the place performing and acting and chasing Medallion Status, and some of the things I learned from them that might be helpful should you visit them.

AKRON, OHIO

Akron is called Rubber City because it is the home of Goodyear Tire. They make and house blimps there, but you will not have time to see them. They have a nice modern public library with a stage where you can make all the blimp jokes you want, finally, and the audience will really laugh and get it. Then a guy will start telling you from the audience the difference between an actual blimp and what Goodyear is building now in nearby Suffield, which is a technically a semi-rigid dirigible. You won't mind this interruption. It's interesting, and it kills time. If you ask them, the audience will make the sound of a semi-rigid dirigible passing overhead (a sound they have all heard) and the whole room will hum. After the show there is a bar on South Main Street called The Lockview that serves grilled cheese sandwiches and slices of deep-fried pepperoni, which is good. The man who brings you there will tell you about how he used to play in showcases with DEVO back when they were starting out, but now he works at the library.

BURLINGTON, VERMONT

If you are backstage at the Higher Ground Ballroom in Burlington, Vermont, you may be asked if you want to meet Mike Gordon. You probably know who Mike Gordon is, but I didn't. When I said I didn't know who Mike Gordon was, people got confused and upset. It was like I had denied ever seeing the sun in the sky. It turns out that Mike Gordon is the bassist for the band Phish. People are very passionate about Phish, especially in Burlington, Vermont, which is where Phish was founded.

Once I was set straight I said, yes, I would be happy to meet Mike Gordon. I was brought to the outer dressing room where Mike Gordon was munching on some catering. I shook his hand, and we tried to make conversation. He's only a little older than me, and also a dad, and I got the feeling that he wasn't sure exactly who I was either, or why he was out on a cold weeknight to see me. I didn't know that he was from Boston and his dad owned the chain of Store 24 convenience stores where I used to buy Moon Knight comics and chocolate milk. I didn't know he went to Lincoln-Sudbury Regional High School, just like a fellow clarinetist I knew from my high school chamber music days, Charlotte. I didn't know Mike Gordon and I shared a birthday.

I mean I didn't know these things until today, years later, because I Googled him just now to make sure I had remembered his name correctly. (I hadn't. I thought it was Phil.) I wish I had known all these things. I could have asked him if it was true, as Charlotte once told me, that all the kids at their school called it "Drinkin' Drugsbury Reasonably High School." But still, he was very nice, and I enjoyed meeting him. When you're in Burlington, and a member of Phish drops by, you have to pay your respects.

This goes for any town and any member of Phish, or that town's Phish equivalent. But you don't have to accept marijuana from the club employee who tells you that everyone refers to him as Captain Weed. Even though it makes him sad, you can politely decline. That time in your life is over now.

CHAPEL HILL, NORTH CAROLINA

The best part about touring is of course meeting the audience after the show. Sometimes they bring you little gifts. Some of these are easy to accept and transport to the next city. They are flat, like zines and comics, or soft and light and packable, like a crocheted hot dog that reads "this is not a sandwich." Other gifts are heavy or breakable. Sometimes they bring you a bottle of very fancy gin that you do not want. They don't understand that you are going to get on a plane in five hours, and that you cannot waltz into the airport with a bottle of gin under your arm no matter what your Medallion Status is. Also, they always bring the fancy super-botanical gins you don't like. They are just being kind, and it's part of the happy price you pay for being a public figure who talks about gin all the time without specifying a brand. For your reference, Plymouth is great, but Beefeater is also fine.

But being a middle-aged imitation stand-up comedian on tour is not the same thing as being an attractive musician on tour. The outlier of Captain Weed aside, no one in any of my audiences has ever offered me drugs, for example. Even during the height of my brief, middle-aged fascination with marijuana edibles, people would not take the hint. The hint being me onstage saying, "GIVE ME MARIJUANA PILLS."

But after my show at the beautiful Carolina Theatre in Raleigh, something happened. A young man and woman shyly approached me in the lobby. The young woman looked over one shoulder and then the other. She pressed an envelope into my hand. It was suggestively lumpy.

"This is just a little gift for the road," she said.

It was happening! Drugs were happening! My neck got hot. I tried to be cool. "Thank you!" I said as I shoved the envelope deep into my pocket. Then I signed her book and they left.

I was afraid to take the envelope out of my pocket. I got to the restaurant where my friends David Rees and Phil Morrison were waiting for me, holding a table. David is a cartoonist, TV host, and artisanal pencil sharpener who was performing and traveling with me, and Phil had directed the series of computer ads that made me famous enough to be both an imitation stand-up comedian and imitation actor. They're both from North Carolina, and they love it there.

"You guys!" I whisper-screamed as I sat down. "Someone gave me drugs, I think!"

They were not as excited as I was. I think they were worried about me. I took out the envelope and opened it carefully. Inside there was a very nice letter and no drugs. It was just a bunch of prepackaged lens wipes for my eyeglasses.

"I thought you could use these on tour," she wrote.

I pushed the lens wipes away from me in panic and disgust, as if the envelope had been stuffed with a mummified cat's paw or something equally inexplicable. How could she have misunderstood what I was asking for? How could I have misunderstood her obviously shifty demeanor? Was she playing a joke on me?

It would be the same if she had said, "I have a very special cigarette for you. But don't smoke it here. Take it back to your hotel and then unroll it, and you will see it's actually a fifty-foot-long microscopic crossword puzzle!" Or: "Come into this back alley and inhale something from this paper bag with me. It contains the dying breath of Thomas Edison!"

But a gift is a gift. The truth is, I did not need drugs. I

certainly needed lens wipes, and I used them for the rest of the tour. And she knew this somehow. Thank you, whoever you are.

By the way, the restaurant we went to was Lantern in Chapel Hill, and you should go there. It's wonderful and it stays open late.

COCOA BEACH, FLORIDA

In Cocoa Beach, Florida, there is a hotel that has a whole surf shop in it. If you do not know what a surf shop is, it is a shop in a strip mall on Cocoa Beach that very rarely sells surfing supplies, but mostly sells clothing to cool young kids who want to stop looking cool and instead look like young Guy Fieri, and old dudes who do want to look cool but will settle for looking like weird dad Jason Mraz. I fell into the latter category. Every now and then, usually while traveling, I figure I will try again and see if I look good in electric blue polo shirts or swimming trunks or jeans. It never works, but you have to keep trying.

When I say this hotel had a surf shop, that is backward. The surf shop had a hotel. The shop was this huge, lofty, warehouse-style retail space, and they had some extra room, so they just took a corner of it and put a Four Points by Sheraton in it. It was as if Costco had built a bed-and-breakfast in a full Victorian mansion in the back, over by the kitty litter pallets.

Half the rooms in the hotel had windows that looked directly into the surf shop. That was their view. These were mirrored, one-way windows, so I could not see in. But I knew the people behind them could see out, as much as they probably didn't want to. Behind every window I could picture a person calling down to the front desk.

"Yes, hi," they would be saying, "Do you have any other rooms available? Any other rooms in the world?... No? I see. Well then, can you please send up a paintbrush and a can of black paint? That's right. Pitch-black. Because I would rather paint these windows black than look at this surf shop. It is depressing enough to look at the surf shop during the day. But at night, when all I have to look at is the security guy getting high in the flip-flop aisle, it makes me sad. It makes me feel like, between the two of us, he is making the better life choices. Oh, but who am I kidding? I do not know if it is day or night because I live in a surf shop and time has no meaning anymore. So never mind the black paint. I'm just going to smash open the window so I can jump out of it. I would rather plunge to my death than spend another minute here. Tell my family they can look for my body in the decorative tank of moray eels just below me in the Sharkpit Bar and Grille, which is also in the surf shop, next to the Starbucks."

Oh, I forgot to mention, there was a bar inside the surf shop as well, called the Sharkpit. And it was right next to a Starbucks. There were no walls, not even a transition in the carpeting, to distinguish them. It was as if some cataclysm had happened, some collapse of time and space, where all these stores had been in their proper dimensions, but then the large hadron collider exploded and they all got compressed into this one space, and also dinosaurs are wandering around and zeppelins are crashing into sputniks and cavemen wearing cowboy hats are riding motorcycles.

So I did not want to shop in this surf shop, because I knew that in those hotel rooms, someone might be trying to make love, and I did not want them to have to look over and see me trying on a rash guard.

But that was OK, because directly across the street was *another* surf shop. It wasn't even across the street, just a skip across a narrow pedestrian breezeway leading to the beach. And *this* surf shop never closes. The Ron Jon Surf Shop of Cocoa Beach is open twenty-four hours. And I can tell you, when you are in your forties, and you are shopping for cool clothes at midnight, buzzed on a blue martini from the Sharkpit next door, it turns out that you are making *all* the right life choices.

BIRMINGHAM, ALABAMA

If you drive into Birmingham from Atlanta, you may still see a billboard. It's stark white with black lettering that simply reads: ANTI-RACIST IS CODE FOR ANTI WHITE. I don't know if it's still there.

I have performed in Birmingham twice. The first time was in 2012, when I was invited to do some comedy with some other *Daily Show* people. The show was called the Daily Show Stand-Up Tour. It would be easy to think that such a tour would feature Jon Stewart. Certainly the audiences thought that, but they were wrong. It was just me and Al Madrigal and Adam Lowitt, a producer on the show. But even though we cruelly tricked them, the people of Birmingham were kind. They laughed hard and filled up all two thousand seats in the auditorium. I was amazed at the size of the crowd. Later, I met and talked to them. They told me how far they had driven. I saw the grateful shine in their eyes. And I realized, Oh! *These are the liberals! These are all the two thousand liberals who live in Alabama, and they all came here to breathe.*

So I came back a few years later to perform at the Bottletree, the cool indie rock club in town. David Rees and I drove in from Atlanta and met up with Jason Sims. Jason lives in Huntsville, Alabama. He grew up in the Huntsville punk rock scene when it existed, and then raised some sons and now calls into podcasts (like mine) and is very funny and charming. He was working on a stand-up act, and I asked him to open for me.

The afternoon before the show, he showed us around town. He pointed out the fifty-six-foot cast-iron statue of the Roman god Vulcan standing at his forge. He looms above the skyline holding a spear he has just made to the sky, reminding Birmingham of its history as a steel and iron town. When Jason was growing up, the spear used to be a torch with an electric light in it. If the torch glowed green, it meant there had been no traffic fatalities in Birmingham that day. If it glowed red, there had been at least one. We mused as to what a Birminghamian was supposed to do with that information.

Then Jason took us to see another, stranger statue called *The Storyteller* outside a Methodist church in the Five Points area. This is a statue of a man with a ram's head reading a mysterious book to a wolf and a dog with a goat on his back, plus five spitting frogs arranged in a pentagram. And oh, the ram's-headed man has a staff with an owl on top of it. This is where all the weirdos and goths and punks used to come and see one another and feel less alone, I was told, before the internet came to town.

The show that night was great. Jason knew Charlie, the woman who booked the show, from his own rock club days, and we all chatted in the cool old RV that functioned as the green room. They spoke about the music scene in the past tense, and there was a feeling that something was disappearing. Then Charlie gave us some T-shirts that had been made by a couple of cool guys with a cool design shop called Yellowhammer. The T-shirts were very soft. One depicted the statue of Vulcan, and the other read "We're glad to have you in Birmingham." I put it on. It felt great, and I did feel glad to be had.

The room that night was packed, I suspect, with the children of all the liberals in Alabama. Jason did a very funny bit about George R. R. Martin that everyone liked. On the televisions above the bar they were showing David Lynch's *Dune*. I could see the third-stage Guild Navigator sceneplaying as I performed. I was home. My one complaint was that I was told I probably shouldn't sing "Rocky Top," which was my closing song at that time. That's a University of Tennessee song, I was told, and this was a Crimson Tide town. I was a little mad. *I thought you were* cool, I wanted to say. *You're telling me that you live in a town with basically a Church of Satan sculpture in the middle of it, a town with a punk scene and soft T-shirts and* Dune *on the bar TV, that you have all this, but I can't sing "Rocky Top" in a rock club? Because of sports?*

But I didn't say this. There are goths and punks and weirdos and two thousand liberals everywhere, yes. But sometimes they live in a place where the light shines green and welcoming for them, and sometimes it shines red and dangerous, and they must constantly navigate a delicate, tense truce between a welcoming soft T-shirt and a billboard full of hate. Some of them don't have the option to leave that billboard behind them on the way out of the state tomorrow, and some of them wouldn't want to. So Jason and I closed with a duet of "Nothing Compares 2 U," and after the show we all went to Al's Deli and Grill for all-night gyros and baked potatoes the size of small dogs. I haven't seen Jason since then. The Bottletree closed, and I hope that doesn't mean that the billboard won that particular fight with the soft T-shirt. Al's is still open though. It was good,

ATHENS, OHIO

If you go to do comedy with Jordan Klepper at Ohio University on Dads Weekend, you should be prepared to see a LOT of dads.

The streets will be full of them before your show. They will be wearing fleece vests with mutual fund logos on them, but don't let that fool you. They are there to party. After your show, the entrance to every bar and restaurant will be clogged with dads lining up to get drunk with their sons because they think this will make them briefly less sad. So here's a tip: go to Casa Nueva. This is where the local Ohio oddballs and theater kids go for late-night Mexican food and beer, and they keep the dads and undergrads away with a five-dollar cover and live, experimental jazz.

I met one of the coolest people on earth in Athens. Before the show, Jordan and I were exploring the town and found ourselves on a side street full of small houses that had been beaten up by years of undergraduate parties. A dadless student named Morgan was idling down this street when he saw us.

"It's John Hodgman," he said without smiling. "Nice to meet you...*finally*."

He said *finally* with such dripping, sarcastic offense that I wanted to adopt him. But Morgan had no time for dads or Dads Weekend. He was carrying a paper bag with a bottle of rum in it, and another paper bag of groceries.

"What are you going to do today?" I asked.

"Well," he said, holding up his bags, "I'm going to drink this rum and then make corn casserole."

There is no reason to tell this story other than to say I think about Morgan and his corn casserole a *lot*. If you're out there, Morgan, look me up. I miss you, son.

PORTLAND, MAINE

There is another Portland called Portland, Maine. It's like they are trying to trick you. This Portland also is cold and wet and it also has a great independent bookstore that I'm happy to buzz market called Print. And like Portland, Oregon, it is also full of young people with gorgeous tattoos and luxurious beards working in cool bakeries and sustainable restaurants. But this Portland is its own place, and it is worth going to.

The theater I was performing at sent a limousine to the airport to pick me up. This time the driver was not a racist. When you get lucky this way, it is good to ask about your driver's life, because they are real human beings and driving cars tends not to be a lifelong profession, but a turning point. Maybe you will learn, as I did, that your driver, a Latina woman, is actually a social worker. Normally she does not drive a car but instead helps immigrants in Portland's Latinx community access state health and welfare services. She will tell you that there is no work for her right now, because all her clients are hiding. They are not seeking health care or leaving their homes because there is a new president and they are afraid they will be arrested, and then it will not feel good to ride in a limousine

KANSAS CITY, MISSOURI

Kansas City is a wonderful town with great barbecue and very nice people. It is also the home to a big celebrity charity event organized by Paul Rudd and Jason Sudeikis and Rob Riggle and their adorable moms, who are all from there. It's called the Big Slick. Paul and Jason and Rob invite all their famous friends to come take part in various events to raise money for the children's hospital. You play in a bowling tournament, you play in a charity softball game, and you do a big show in a beautiful theater, and it's all a lot of fun.

But the best part of the weekend is going to visit the sick children and their families at the hospital. It is humbling and inspiring to see the strength with which these families are coping with the aftermath of the worst news of their lives and the uncertain future they are facing together. It is also a helpful tool to measure exactly how somewhat famous you still are. The answer is: not very somewhat famous.

Time after time, I entered hospital rooms full of blank confused stares, people who were waiting for Paul Rudd but instead got me. Time after time, the weary parents would say something like, "Here is our daughter Megan. She just got out of chemo, so she's pretty weak."

And you have to look into that child's worried and confused eyes and say, "Hi, Megan. It's John Hodgman. I was in some television ads when you were two and I have a very small column in the *New York Times Magazine*. You don't know about those things? That's fine. Maybe you saw me on television as the Hitler impersonator or the deranged psychiatrist at the racist turn-of-the-century hospital? No? Do you remember my joke on *The Daily Show* about economics being called the Dismal Science because it was named for Sir Eustace Dismal? Hey, Megan, did you know that even though I wrote a lot of my segments, I wasn't officially a writer on the show, so I was never eligible for an Emmy award? Isn't that a funny story? No? Oh!

Maybe you heard me on *WTF* when Marc Maron and I talked about Walter Benjamin and authenticity in the age of mechanical reproduction? No? Huh. How do you feel about extinct hockey?"

And then after a while the parents would come back over and say, "Please stop. Stop this. Don't you understand? Our world has been turned inside out and then exploded into unrecognizable shards of pain, and every day we worry that this might be the last day with our child. It is not a comfort to have a random person from television that we don't recognize come in. This isn't helping. Actually it is increasing our pain and confusion. Your lack of fame is actually hurting us."

Obviously these conversations were never said out loud, only in our eyes.

It wasn't just me. I walked the hospital floor with Haley Joel Osment for a while. I had not met Haley Joel Osment before. He is an incredibly sweet person, so the children enjoyed his presence even though they had no idea who he was. And Haley Joel Osment understood this. He very happily just said, "I've worked on some video games," and then asked the children about their lives. But the parents knew who Haley Joel Osment was, and honestly, I'm not sure that if you're a parent of a sick child, you want to see Haley Joel Osment wandering around the children's ward.

Everyone loved seeing Paul Rudd, of course, because he is one of the most loveable humans on earth. But the *most* famous, cheering, and welcome visitor by a Kansas City mile was

Weird Al Yankovic, zero question. When Weird Al walked into a room, every eye would beam and every face would break into happy recognition and excitement, both parents and kids. Because Weird Al is a wonderful person who also is truly, intergenerationally famous. When Weird Al was in the room, the lame walked and the blind saw.

Art can be challenging or moving or unsettling. It can offer an awakening and it can offer solace. But I think art's best value is that it is distracting. Weird Al let everyone think about something else that day, specifically Weird Al, which is a great thing to think about. I hope even my presence was something to break up the day, to interrupt the monotony of dread and worry and replace it with something, anything else for a moment—a little mystery they could solve. I also hope Megan checks out my three-episode arc on *Red Oaks*. It's a great show, and Paul Reiser should have won an Emmy for it.

NORTHAMPTON, MASSACHUSETTS, AND BOSTON, MASSACHUSETTS

If you're doing a show with Jonathan Coulton at the Calvin Theater in Northampton, make sure to check the marquee. It might be that you'll see that the musician Lyle Lovett is playing there the next night. You won't be able to see him, because you're playing Boston tomorrow, but you can tweet him, like I did: "I feel sad for Lyle Lovett that there will be no more stage for him tomorrow after Jonathan Coulton and I DESTROY IT TONIGHT."

Then maybe Lyle Lovett will tweet back: "Please leave me a little something to work with at the Calvin tomorrow night. Thanks for the mention."

This will be very exciting for you, because you used to love playing "Here I Am" on your college radio show, and you will explain all of this to Jonathan on the drive to Boston and he will be totally, totally fascinated to hear more stories of when you worked at the radio station.

When you check into your hotel in Boston, Jonathan will leave because he is going to stay with his in-laws to be polite and save money. You will try to explain to him that touring is hard and draining. You can't mix in bread-and-butter visits with family. Sometimes you have to splurge. But he is too nice and says: see you at the show.

Then, when you're waiting for the elevator to take you up to your room, the elevator door will open, and Lyle Lovett will be standing inside it. It will be so strange and surreal for both of you that your brains will reject the strangeness and pretend that it is real. "It's John Hodgman!" Lyle Lovett will say, like you are old friends. He will explain that he just played Boston and was now about to hit the road for Northampton to play there tonight. He and you are on the same tour, but in reverse, meeting only at this miraculous inflection point that Jonathan Coulton missed, just to save a little money.

"I loved you in *Bored to Death*," Lyle Lovett will say. "Make sure you put that in your book!"

Actually, now that I think of it, it is very unlikely that this will happen to you. Statistically almost impossible. But if you want to try, stay at the Hotel Northampton in Northampton and the Four Seasons in Boston. That's right: the Four Seasons. The road is hard, and you have to splurge on yourself from time to time, if you can.

AUSTIN, TEXAS

Speaking of splurging, if you arrive in Austin, Texas, at the end of a long tour, I highly recommend staying at the Inter-Continental Stephen F. Austin hotel, if you can. It is walking distance to the Paramount Theatre, which is one of the nicest places to perform. There is also a parking garage to the hotel that houses a tiny bar behind a blank door. They have good food and good drinks that are served over gigantic, perfectly transparent ice cubes that are cut and polished lovingly by a young man with earrings.

The hotel is also very nice. It has a lap pool in the basement that you can swim back and forth in like a depressed polar bear and freak out the older couple who is trying to have a date in the hot tub.

But here is some advice: if you check into the hotel at the end of a long tour and you immediately just want to drop your bag and run over to the $9 mini can of Pringles next to the ice bucket and shove all those Pringles in your mouth, go ahead and do that. That has become a ritual by now. However, if you discover that, this time, the Pringles can is already open and all the Pringles have been eaten except, weirdly, for two, do not get mad. Do not pace in a hot fury and then finally break down and call the front desk. Do not tell them that this is unacceptable. Do not explain to them that they have failed in their primary mission, which is not merely fresh Pringles every day. It is to trick you into believing that this hotel room had never existed before you opened the door, that it was conjured from some sterile dimension out of nothingness, and certainly no one had ever, *ever* masturbated in it before.

Don't do that: what I did. Put down the phone. Keep your cool. In a moment you are about to stand onstage in front of people who paid money to see you. On tour you have seen things and had adventures that you will never forget. Yes, you are frayed at every edge of your being and missing your family, but you were the one who chose to do this. And the good news is that it is not your job to clean up Pringles cans and dirty sheets. Don't get mad and mean. Everyone is doing what they have to do, and everyone is doing the best they can. And soon you will be going home.

(Oh yes, and *obviously* leave a tip for your chambermaid. Five dollars every day. If you forget to get change and only have a twenty, leave the twenty. It won't hurt you. It will feel great.)

Chapter Six

THE SPORT OF
MARBLE KINGS

I have mentioned extinct hockey a few times now, and you deserve an explanation. It is the only sport that I follow. Growing up in Boston without liking sports was an isolating experience. People in Boston like sports a *lot*, and they yell at you if you don't. But honestly, the worst bullying I received around sports was once I was grown up and chatting nicely about David Lynch or *Star Blazers* or whatever with other adult male nerds. These were my people, fellow pasty men with glasses, and I thought I could trust them. But then I would casually let it slip that I didn't know anything about baseball, for example, and these men would explode. They would rain shame upon me. It's not about the running and batting and throwing, they would say. It's about the narrative, the mythic accomplishments and ancient rivalries, the grand histories of the athletes and their teams and their cities. It's about the *stories*, these sports nerds would repeat on and on, seeming to forget that books and movies already exist.

But then, some years ago in my distant early forties, something changed. It was an early summer evening. I was walking on my block in Brooklyn, and a young man with a beard rode by on a fixed-gear bicycle. I noticed him because we do not get many young hipster incursions in Park Slope. This is primarily middle-aged-mom-and-dad territory. But he didn't startle me so much as his forearm startled me, and specifically his forearm tattoo of the logo of the Hartford Whalers.

The Hartford Whalers were a hockey team. They were in the NHL—the only major league sports team to ever play in Connecticut. I knew just enough about New England sports to know this, and just enough to know that the team had always struggled and finally left Hartford in 1997 to become a different hockey team. And I knew their logo: A green W, capped with a wide whale's tail.

I went to college in the '90s, and remember then how black students started wearing baseball hats featuring the logo of old Negro league baseball teams. They were commemorating a tragically overlooked cultural legacy. Sometimes white dudes would also wear Negro league hats around this time. I am so so so lucky I never made that mistake. But now in Park Slope, it occurred to me that having a hipster forearm tattoo of a defunct hockey team was the whitest version of this reclaiming of a forgotten history.

I had not thought about that logo for twenty years, but I had always liked it. It had a bold, graphic, seventies feel. It makes sense, because it was in fact designed in 1979 by a graphic designer in Connecticut named Peter Good. He had never designed a sports identity before (or since), and he and his wife, Jan Cummings Good, are still creating clean, unfussy logos for local restaurants, museum exhibitions, and folk and chamber music festivals. You can check them out at cummings-good .com, and you really should, because it was not until I went home that night and saw all of Good's sketches for the Whalers logo that I realized what he had hidden in it, and I gasped out loud.

It's dumb to describe the visual language of a perfect logo, but in case you don't have the internet in front of you, I will try. The whale's tail nestles into the W, completing the center rise of the W, but not *quite* completing it, leaving a little bar of white to form a negative space, a nothingness that you would miss until someone shows you that it's in the shape of an empty H. *H for Hartford*. That is when I gasped, and I've heard many gasps since, after I've pointed it out to people, even people who like sports. *How could I have missed it?* we have all said. The Hartford Whalers' is not only the best logo in extinct hockey, but all of sports. And I will fight you over this in a sports bar if you disagree. Get out of here with your old-school Milwaukee Brewers logo. Yeah, I see the M and the B hidden in that baseball mitt. It's obvious. It's dumb. It's nowhere near the clean, classic ingenuity of the Whalers logo. It's childish, is what it is.

I did not want to get a Whalers tattoo, but luckily I had the occasion to fly a few times out of Bradley International (!) Airport in Windsor Locks, Connecticut, which at the time was one of the few places still selling Whalers merchandise. I bought a hat there, and then, on another trip, a second hat. Someone gave me a Whalers T-shirt. My friend Jesse gave me a lapel pin with a Whaler-logoed Zamboni on it. As I bought this stuff, I gradually and accidentally learned about hockey itself, and I discovered I liked it.

Part of my dislike of sports was its celebration of winning. Winning is the goal of most games. But as an X-Men reader in the '80s, I felt more kinship with the outcasts and weirdos and noble losers. That's why I was a Democrat. That's why, while I didn't follow them at all, I never actually *minded* the Red Sox. Their constant struggle to stand up to their bullies, the Yankees, was one sports narrative I could half appreciate, especially because the Red Sox always choked and lost. These were my people. Once they won the World Series though, they lost me forever. I don't even think they cared.

But in hockey, I now realized, everyone is a loser. It is the minorest of the major league sports, and if you are a fan in the United States, your passion is mostly considered by culture to be a marginal folly. Mostly your teams are failing and relocating and renaming themselves, and even in places like Boston or Chicago with long hockey heritage, your teams are overshadowed by the big-boy sports. If you are a hockey fan, you are always something of a person without a country, and that country you are without is Canada.

But do not feel bad. At least you are not a professional hockey player, punished both on the ice and off with brutal hits and low pay. Unless you are one of the few hockey superstars, chances are, you come from a small town in Canada, skated back and forth in the dim limelight of hockey semi-stardom for a while, got injured a bunch of times, eventually aged out of the game, and, with comparatively few endorsement opportunities and comparatively few jobs within the comparatively small pro-hockey back offices and media, went back to your home in rural Canada and, I hope, are living a happy retirement there. I hope you do not spend a lot of time looking out over the cold plains of Manitoba saying to yourself, *Did that happen? Did hockey actually happen to me?*

And as sad as hockey is, *extinct* hockey is even sadder, smaller, and more human. One of my favorite pieces of Hartford memorabilia that I found was the *1979 Hartford Whalers Wives 1990–91 Cookbook and Family Album.* It's a small, xeroxed, plastic-ring-bound book compiled and sold to benefit the University of Connecticut's children's cancer fund. There is Peter Good's logo on the cover, but otherwise it has all the design panache of a drying machine manual. Here is Ron and Mary Lou Francis's recipe for Steak and Mushrooms à la Ronnie. Here is Bab's Chili and Holly's Meatballs and Sherri's Shrimp Dip and a different cream cheese dip called Pete's Cold Pizza. There are *two* different recipes for Spaghetti Pie, one from the Ladouceurs, the other from the Petersons, staring each other down across pages 50 and 51. I would like to get to the bottom of that feud. Then Jeannie Leach drops in with Spaghetti *Salad* on the very next page: a bold combination of thin spaghetti, two cans of shrimp, two bottles of Catalina dressing, scallions, and green peppers that changes the spaghetti game forever. "Best," says Jeannie in the instructions, "if served the next day."

They are all unfussy, thrifty meals, and the recipes are accompanied by photos of all the young hockeyists and their wives and children. They are all in 1991 clothes and hair smiling gamely on lumpy sofas or crowded into tiny kitchens around electric ranges. There is no glamour here, just young people leading transient lives and hoping for the best. Here is Scott Young sitting on a counter peeling a banana. Here is Carey Wilson on his back, smiling as he takes a wrench to his garbage disposal. Here is Mike Tomlak, just talking on the phone. Here is Kay Whitmore, staring into his refrigerator. It's my favorite sports action shot.

Suddenly, I got it. I understood what all those pasty baseball men were trying to tell me. If sports is about the stories, this cookbook is the best collection of Raymond Carver short fiction I've ever read, and I love them all.

At one point I began to wonder: Is it possible that I would like actual hockey? I decided to find out when I was dared to go to an actual hockey game for a podcast called *Surprisingly Awesome* by the show's producer Rachel Ward. I confess I was curious to experience real-life hockey. Rachel got us tickets to a game in Pittsburgh between the Penguins and another team. I just had to check my notes to remember who the opposing team was. It was the Tampa Bay Lightning, but I will just call them THE ENEMIES. Even though it was a playoff game, it was not that hard to get tickets.

Before going, I contacted Greg Wyshynski, a hockey fan and blogger I know who once beat me in a movie-trivia game. I wanted to ask him if it would be inappropriate for me to wear my Hartford Whalers hat in the arena. I knew that Ron Francis had played for Pittsburgh after he left the Whalers, so probably there were no hard feelings. But I wasn't sure if there were any old rivalries I should know about that would trigger sensitive sports fans and prompt them to yell at or punch me. He told me I would be fine. Most people have fond memories of the Whalers. Then he told me about the time he had gone to a New Jersey Devils game as a child and a woman got mad at his nine-year-old sister and poured beer on her. This was a fond memory for him.

Greg also told me about a superstition he had grown up with: he had to drink pink lemonade at the hockey game or his team would lose. I was offended by this, and not merely because I believe in science. I may not like sports, but I have deep respect for athletes, not merely because they can hurt me, but also because they accomplish amazing things through hard training. Don't insult them by saying that you can control them with your mind and your drink choice, Greg.

I did bring my Whalers hat to Pittsburgh, but I covered my bets and bought a Penguins hat when I was down there. It was a replica cap with their '70s logo on it, a blocky, skating penguin holding a hockey stick. It wasn't exactly extinct hockey, but it was close. What I really wanted was a Pittsburgh Pirates hat. That was the name of the first pro hockey team in Pittsburgh, unaffiliated with the baseball team of that name. But I could find no Hockey Pirates merch anywhere, not even at the Western Pennsylvania Sports Museum, where I spent the afternoon before the game.

The Hockey Pirates logo was an off-kilter yellow P on a black field, the first to use the color scheme that is now shared by all Pittsburgh sports teams. The Penguins colors *used* to be black and white and ice blue, which is appropriate for a team called the Penguins, but not as good for the Pittsburghian mania for sports-design consistency. But when the Penguins wanted to switch to yellow and black, the Boston Bruins sued them, claiming it was too close to their own colors. Luckily, the Hockey Pirates were there to save the day. The Penguins used the Hockey Pirates logo to prove historical precedence and won the lawsuit. For playing such an important role in Pittsburgh sports history, you'd think the Western Pennsylvania Sports Museum would have more than just one single hockey program from a Hockey Pirates game against the Ottawa Senators in 1930. But that's just the kind of disrespect the sport of extinct hockey gets.

But to their vast credit, the museum *did* have a display case dedicated to Doug Opperman, the boy who won the citywide marbles championship multiple times in the 1930s. They had some of his original marbles and his marbles bag and the crown he was awarded, which itself was made of marbles. They also had the white sweater vest he wore with the words "PITTS-BURGH, PA MARBLE KING" on it. I really wanted to steal it. I wanted to steal it as a gift to the hipster with the Whalers tattoo on his arm as a thank-you for sending me on this journey. I mean: what a look that would be!

Finally, I couldn't spend any more time with the Marble King, so I went to the hockey game. And do you know what? I LIKED IT. We walked to the stadium. It was reasonably sized and unflashy, like hockey itself. There were no sky boxes or luxury suites that I could see. We all just walked in and took our seats around the tall, deep hockey pit. At the top of the pit it was basically a food court. Down below, they threw about a hundred pucks on the ice and the players warmed up by shooting them around. It looked like an accident had happened and there was no one else to clean up this puck spill, so might as well get the professional athletes to do it. It was homey and I felt at home.

Throughout the game a person dressed as a penguin would pop up in various parts of the arena, bang on a soup pot, and chant: "LET'S GO PENS. LET'S GO PENS." It was a pretty rudimentary chant, in an almost brutally basic 1-2-3 rhythm suitable for the 99 percent Caucasian crowd. Linguistically speaking, the chant really should have been "LET'S GO *PENGS*." But I chose not to point this out to the people around me in the stands.

Hockey players are amazing. I didn't appreciate it until I saw it in person. Ice skating on its own requires a tremendous amount of dexterity, endurance, and grace. Your body is working hard just to not finish falling to the ground all the time, and then someone hands you a stick and says, "Go backward and hit that round hard rubber thing... oh, never mind. It's gone now. Sorry you just got punched, BTW." The game is fast and impossible. It is a game of intensely watching things *almost* happen, only to be frustrated at the last second. And this tension increases and increases and increases, and when the impossible thing (a goal) does happen, it's like you've witnessed a quantum event. You jump up and you chant, "LET'S GO PENS! LET'S GO PENS!"

The only problem is that the other team can also get goals. Pretty soon the Enemies were up a bit, and then the Penguins came back, and the chanting continued and then the teams were tied. Unlike extinct hockey, the outcome of actual hockey is not known, and this is unbearable. As the third period ended in a tie, my experience began to turn. Until 2006, the NHL allowed games to end in a tie, which seemed a gracious, Canadian way to prevent anyone from getting too excited, and also to let people who had had enough hockey go home at a reasonable hour. But now, at the end of the third period, our beloved Pens and the Enemies were tied 3-3, and so began Sudden Death. Whoever scored first would win.

After 105 full minutes of hockey and breaks and hockey and breaks and hockey, I was freezing and emotionally exhausted. My senses were all full of hockey, and that penguin I used to like and chant with now seemed like a demon. I wanted it to be over, and I wanted the Penguins to win. Suddenly, I remembered Greg's pink lemonade trick. And even though I still believed in science, I became possessed of an equally powerful conviction, a deep reptile instinct, that if I took off my Penguins hat and put on my Whalers hat, the Penguins would win. The universe would *know* that I had been led from that hipster tattoo to this hat to this town, not just to watch but to participate in the victory of this team, while meanwhile transforming into an actual sports fan and a whole, normal human. It was obvious that the Whalers hat would help the Penguins win. They are both marine animals! Because it's not just about sports. It's about the story.

Obviously, the Penguins lost. About seven seconds after I put on my Whalers hat, the Tampa Bay Enemies scored, and the game was over. It was so sudden, I didn't even know it was over. There was not a single groan of defeat among the Penguins fans around me. The entire arena went dead silent, and in my memory it just went dark. As I sat there in the darkened arena, I felt sad for the hockey players and the people of Pittsburgh, because I had misread the omens and caused this to happen. Some might take that as evidence of magical thinking verging on mental illness, but I was convinced. I stay away from real hockey now. It's better for both of us.

But I still love extinct hockey. It's not just the Whalers. I also follow the California Golden Seals and the Minnesota North Stars, and I am always on the lookout for an Atlanta Flames or Michigan Stags hat. There's a team for everyone: there's just that much failure in hockey! For a while a man named Gene would come to my shows and give me hats of increasingly obscure old teams and tell me their sad tales: the Vancouver Millionaires fell to the Toronto St. Patricks before becoming the Vancouver Maroons for two seasons before disbanding. The Brooklyn Americans played a single season. The Montreal Wanderers never recovered as a team after their stadium burned down.

And it's a growing sport. It's very common to see the Whalers logo these days, not just in Connecticut airports. And the Carolina Hurricanes (which I know now is the team the Whalers became) will occasionally have throwback nights and deck out their hockeyists in full Whalers uniforms. I suspect some of this renaissance has to do with the legion of devoted middle-aged Connecticutians who miss their team and still talk about them all the time on the internet. But I assign most of the credit to the timeless power of Peter Good's logo and also my psychic powers.

Now that the Whalers logo was cool and popular again, I wondered if the man on the fixed-gear bike regretted his tattoo. Hipsterism is the purposeful cultivation of uncool and esoteric tastes, and sometimes a shortcut to that aesthetic is to embrace the ugly. Did that guy now wish he had gotten the logo of the Quebec Nordiques tattooed on his arm instead? Because if the Whalers have the best logo in sports, the Nordiques unquestionably had the worst.

Where the negative-space H of the Whalers logo engages and invites you in, the Nordiques logo slams the door in your face in a way that leaves you confused and upset. "What the hell?" you want to say to the Nordiques logo. "I was just walking by! I wasn't even going to knock!"

That's how I felt one day in Montreal when I first saw a Nordiques hat far, far in the back of a souvenir shop near the Cathedral. The shop only had one of them, as I remember. Maybe they were compelled by Canadian law to have it there. I loved it.

I won't make you go look at my Nordiques hat. It is beyond human perception. It is supposed to be about three-quarters of a blood-red igloo, bisected at an angle by an incredibly thin-armed, fat-bladed hockey stick with a spherical puck on top of it. And this bisection of the blood-red igloo is supposed to form a lowercase N. But no one sees this. Most people see some kind of abstract, mutated elephant.

Like the Whalers, the Nordiques were founded in 1972 as part of the World Hockey Association. And like the Whalers, they were absorbed into the NHL in 1979. And like the Whalers, they never played really good hockey. In 1991, as Jeannie Leach was blowing up Hartford minds with Spaghetti Salad, the Quebec Nordiques came in last in the league. Nabbing the first-round draft pick, they chose Eric Lindros, a rising young hockey talent from London, Ontario. Everyone in Quebec City was excited. Lindros was going to turn the team around.

But Eric Lindros was not excited. Eric Lindros said, "No."

Quebec City said, *"Mais bien sur! Il faut que vous jouez au hockey au Quebec! C'est le loi de hockey!"*

But Eric Lindros said, "I don't even know what you're saying. No." He didn't want to move to a small, cold city where they only spoke French. Eric Lindros would prefer not to play hockey at all than to play for the Nordiques. And for a whole year, he didn't.

Finally the Nordiques gave up. They traded Lindros to the Philadelphia Flyers, where he was happy to play hockey and would do so for years. To give you a sense of how valuable Lindros was as a player, the Flyers gave the Nordiques *five* other hockey players to get him, plus $15 million in cash. *United States* dollars.

But it turned out, these five players were very good. Suddenly, the Nordiques started to win. That season they went to the playoffs for the first time in six years. Quebec was excited. It was finally all turning around! But then the owner ran out of money and sold the team to Denver, where they became the Colorado Avalanche. That first year in Colorado, they won the Stanley Cup. They were the same team, the same players. The only difference was that they weren't in Quebec, and they weren't wearing that deformed elephant on their sweaters anymore, because the Nordiques no longer existed.

And that is how the Quebec Nordiques beat the Hartford Whalers to win the Sadness Cup, the highest honor in extinct hockey. And yes, hockey uniform shirts are called sweaters, because hockey is adorable.

As with my Hartford Whalers hat, I was occasionally stopped on the street by people who remembered the team and the logo and wanted to talk about it. But if the people who remembered the Whalers were wistful, the Nordiques people seemed traumatized. They would look at my hat like they were recovering a painful memory they had long repressed.

"Nordiques?" they would say.

"Yes," I would say.

"Wow," they would say. "What was that logo supposed to be? An elephant?"

"No," I would say. And then I would explain it to them. This happened again and again on street corners and at rest stops. I should note that no one ever said, "It's John Hodgman! Why are you wearing that hat?" They only cared about the hat. This was how I began to realize I was no longer as famous as the saddest extinct foreign sports team.

Still, that made me just famous enough to be invited to host an awards gala for science fiction and fantasy novelists, and so I did. The ceremony was held at a hotel in Chicago, and it was fun. I got to meet a lot of authors who I admired and hang out with them at the bar. The science fiction and fantasy authors didn't party as hard as, say, the violin section of the Boston Pops, as I would later learn, but we had a good time. None of them got mad at me for not liking baseball. They were real nerds writing actual stories that they made up in their minds.

For my speech, I wrote this line, which I think may be the last actual pure joke I ever wrote:

"My favorite kind of science fiction is post-apocalyptic dystopia. But I just heard at the bar that genre is going out of style. Frankly, that's not a future I want to live in."

This destroyed.

While we were there, the hotel was also hosting a high school prom. At one point we were all on the same floor. One ballroom was full of science fiction and fantasy novelists, ages thirty-five to roughly immortal. At the other end of the hall was a ballroom full of eighteen-year-olds dancing to extremely popular music. It could not have been more science-fiction-and-fantasy-ish: this hotel hallway was a literal portal between two completely different realities.

I took a break at one point and stepped out into the hallway. I observed the teenagers. They were all very happy and handsome and beautiful and jockish. If there were nerds among them, they had stayed home. The young were dancing so hard that they almost couldn't breathe. They would come out to the hallway to take a break and catch their breath, only to lose it again laughing with each other.

I felt bad for them. Imagine you are eighteen years old and you are going to prom. This is maybe the most glamorous night of your life so far, and you're probably going to hug and kiss someone, maybe that person you've liked for *so long*. And then you step out into the hall for a moment, just a moment, and you see me: this weird bearded withered old man, a dark glimpse into the future of humanity. I think I unsettled the young people. It certainly unsettled the fifty-year-old gym-teacher-type man who was chaperoning them. He held out his hand to me and literally yelled, "No," like Gandalf before the Balrog. "Your people are not here!"

I slunk away to rejoin my people. Just as the doors were

closing, I heard him say, "Wait. Is that a Quebec Nordiques hat?" But it was too late to make amends. The portal between jock and nerd, youth and age, sports and extinct sports had closed behind me.

PS: I did eventually talk to the man with the Whalers tattoo, by the way. After we got back from Pittsburgh, Rachel Ward surprised me by tracking him down and putting me on the phone with him. His name is Scott Tomford, and he runs communications for the New Orleans chapter of the Democratic Socialists of America and tweets at @kidpretentious. He's not a hipster, and his love for the Whalers was not ironic but honest and lifelong since childhood. A true extinct hockey fan. He told me that when he was a kid, he watched them play their very last game in Hartford. He told me they won, and I was glad for them, and him too.

Chapter Seven

DISNEY JAIL

Whenever I was on a break from touring or my television show and heading home, I would make sure to stop at the Hot Wheels section of the airport toy store to get a present for my son. He's not really into cars, but around this time, Hot Wheels was making a lot of superhero-branded toy cars, and I liked bringing him the strangest ones.

Mostly superheroes do not need cars because of webs and powers and so on. Even the Batmobile really only made sense back when it was introduced in 1939, because only about seven people had cars then. You could park a big black car with a bat on it anywhere then. But there is really no reason for the Flash to have a Flash car, unless the Flash wanted to go much slower that day, or he had a bunch of luggage to take with him while crime fighting. There is no reason that the cosmic dictator Darkseid, who can teleport across galaxies in his endless quest for the anti-life equation, also needs a sexy Dream Van XGW with a painting of himself on it to bring dates back to after the state fair closes. That said, it's pretty amazing that he does.

I saw at least two models of an Aquaman car over the years I stopped by the Hot Wheels store, and that made sense. The first was a 1965 Ford Ranchero. The second looked like a submarine on wheels. I wasn't sure whether it was designed to go in the water, or be full *of* water. Either way, Aquaman really *does* need a car. It's great that he can swim so well, but when he gets to Metropolis or wherever, it has to be a drag to once again haul himself up onto some dirty pier way on the edge of town and trudge, freezing and sopping, to the subway. He could probably use a lift and also a cup of cocoa.

But my favorite was the Daredevil car, a 1967 Ford Bronco Roadster with a picture of Daredevil on it that Daredevil would never see, because Daredevil is blind. Of course he has enhanced senses that compensate for his blindness: super-hearing, super-touching and -tasting, a mysterious "radar sense" that might be echolocation, and super-smelling. But I'm still not sure he should be on the road. You can't echolocate a stop light.

Daredevil did not have a car on the television show I had been watching while staying at Paul and Janie's house. Mostly Daredevil just walked around on rooftops and maybe took Ubers. I'm not really sure. Watching *Daredevil*, I began to appreciate what a brutal and boring business being a superhero would be, especially with Daredevil's dumb powers. It's all just climbing up a fire escape to the roof of a Manhattan tenement, waiting around in the cold until you super-hear or super-smell some crime being committed, and then climbing all the way back down to punch someone in the neck and get punched back. What a stupid chore.

Honestly, if I got hit in the eyes with a mystery gas that blinded me but gave me super senses, I don't think I would fight crime. I would probably mostly feel confused and need some therapy. Ultimately, I think I would be happy just to go about my life again. I don't think it would occur to me to keep my new super senses a big secret just so I can punch and kick a bunch of street-level criminals all night long. In fact, I probably would reveal my powers to science so that I could be studied and perhaps bring help to other visually impaired people who *don't* have echolocation. Plus, in the television show, most of the crime in Daredevil's neighborhood of Hell's Kitchen is human trafficking and/or ninja related. I don't see how those guys automatically become my problem just because I can suddenly smell real good.

But let's say I *had* to become a superhero. Let's say it was a law or I had to avenge an uncle or something. If I *were* staying up all night fighting street crime, I don't think I would keep my day job as a storefront neighborhood attorney who mostly works pro bono. Being an attorney is very time-consuming and mentally taxing even when you're being paid well. Probably I would pick a different day job, like data entry or working at a yogurt shop or traffic counting. Just something mindless so I could zone out a little and save up energy for my true passion: punching and getting punched.

But of course in real life, I wouldn't even have much punching to do. It would be boring. Hell's Kitchen is where the *Daily Show* studios are, so I knew it pretty well. We didn't have a lot of human trafficking or ninjas. Mostly we had new, glassy luxury condos and Audi dealerships around us. I looked up the statistics at one point and discovered the most reported crime in the area was the theft of iPads from cars. Probably Hell's Kitchen doesn't need a superhero so much as it needs *more* affordable storefront attorneys helping working poor people to not be unlawfully evicted to make way for more condos. Maybe masked vigilantes should go where they are really needed, like releasing the unredacted Mueller report or helping women get out of fraternity parties. Probably the last thing Hell's Kitchen needs is a blind man driving a 1967 Ford Bronco Roadster navigating by smell.

Anyway, these cars would amuse me so I would always buy one for my son in the hope that it would make up for him not having a father most of the time.

Parents are taught that it takes some time before a child develops object permanence. That's why peekaboo is hilarious, because babies are not very smart. They don't get that when you hide your face behind your hands, your face continues to exist. They think it has disappeared forever.

This confuses the babies, but not for long. They may think, *So sad. Bye bye forever, Face.* But babies get on with their lives. They get right back into it, pushing their tongues out and growing their brains and pooping their pants until: PEEKABOO!

FACE IS BACK!!! Then they are scared out of their minds. *What witchery is this?* science has shown babies to think. But as fear always leads to laughter (except in cases of death or maiming), so the babies' terror eases into the relief and growing understanding that Face is not *back*. Face was always there.

Ha ha, say the babies. *Face will always be there for me. Turns out, it's Hands that are the assholes. Who saw that plot twist coming? Not me. I'm a baby. Oh, look, Face is laughing now. This is a fun game I guess. I wonder whe—AAAGH! FACE, WHERE ARE YOU?!*

Eventually the baby becomes a child and figures it out. Through peekaboo they learn that Face and Hands are permanent objects in space, and you can't trust either of them. Once that happens, parents think they have done their job, but really they have just trained their children to turn away from them and look for security in blankets and Playmobil figures who aren't playing head games with them all the time. This is the best time to start being an imitation comedian and minor television personality who has to travel all the time. Take it from me. When your children are five, six, seven, eight, you can go away for long stretches and then come back again, and do this for years, and they will be fine, because children are resilient. They move past confusing, hurtful changes quickly, and adapt swiftly to each new reality of these lives they cannot control. It will not occur while you are flying through the air, drinking free Fresca in first class, that this resilience is also why children can be kidnapped and so easily trained as soldiers.

However, what parents are *not* taught, but really should be, is that as the child gets older, object *permanence* gives way to a growing sense of *impermanence*. Children feel themselves growing. As they turn nine, ten, eleven, they feel the pain in their shins as their legs lengthen. A little later, hair grows on their arms and legs and elsewhere, and while this werewolf transformation is gentle compared to what you saw in *An American Werewolf in London* (which I only read about in *Starlog* magazine, because I was too scared to see that movie), the children understand, even before puberty, that childhood is leaving them and eventually they will become monsters. That is when children also begin to understand that, yes, Face *can* go away. They wonder why Face keeps going away. They wonder if Face will ever come back.

That's how it was as I was flying back and forth across the country all those times. Our daughter is very competitive, so she will be mad when I say it was hardest on our son. But she was thirteen going on twenty-nine by this time. She was fully confident that she could leave home and live in an apartment on her own and decorate it better than ours, and we knew she was right. While this would have caused legal difficulties for all of us, we might have all been better off if we had let her do it. But my son was nine going on seven, small for his age. He was funny and smart, but a little dreamy, often waking up not knowing what day it was, and still not even sure of the concept of months. At one point, when he was a toddler, I got frustrated about something and yelled, "I quit," and it hurt him very badly.

He thought I had quit being his father. I explained that that was not the case, but I don't think he ever stopped believing it. Now, whenever I came back from a long stretch away, it would take some long, quiet days before he got used to me again. And when I would leave, he would never cry anymore. He would cycle down into an accepting, low-emotion sleep mode.

"I have to go to work," I would say.

"I know," he would say.

"I know it is hard," I would say. "I'm sorry." And I would mean it. But what was the alternative? *Not* being on television? Unacceptable. And so I would ride out to the Sky Lounge and distract myself with its cheeses and liquors and broths until I was once again aloft across the continent.

One time I had been in Los Angeles for several weeks. There was going to be a break in the show and I was going to go home, but then I was offered a small part in *another* television show that was also shooting in Los Angeles. I had to take it: it was a job on television. But because it was my family's spring break, my wife and our children could join me. It was very nice. We rented a house and pretended like we actually lived together for a whole week.

While my family was visiting, I took them all to Disneyland. Because I only had one day off, and because I felt very guilty, we hired a Disney VIP tour guide to walk us around the park. The VIP tour guides are nice young men and women who wear plaid vests and are able to walk you to the front of certain lines. It feels very bad at first, to be so obviously and flagrantly crashing the FastPass line at Splash Mountain. It is hard to look into the faces of the parents and their children who have done nothing but be patient and follow the rules, only to see their spots stolen at the last moment by some dude they absolutely do *not* recognize from *Bored to Death*. What *they* see is just another rich family who have convinced themselves that wealth makes them virtuous and thus deserving of special treatment. In these moments you wonder what you are teaching their kids, and your own. Then you realize you are teaching them the truth about America. And then the log goes down the chute and your son doesn't hate you for a second and the flash goes off as the ride cam takes your photo, a moment of laughing happy joy between the two of you where you do not feel like a monster but instead the greatest dad who has ever lived. And when the log hits the lagoon and the lagoon showers you in tepid park water, you want to go again. And you can, easily, with that VIP guide. Right to the front of the line.

Not only did we get special treatment, but we didn't even pay for regular park admission. Our friend Mark, who was working at the park at the time, walked us in. Mark is an actor. He worked in Frontierland, doing comedy in the Golden Horseshoe Saloon show, in which he played the mayor.

See, son? I wanted to say. *This is what makes all my time away worth it. We are being personally walked into Disneyland by the mayor. Sure, he's just the mayor of* Frontierland, *not of all Disneyland. But we are making connections in the Disneyland political machine!*

At some point as we wandered the park, Mayor Mark mentioned in passing that Disneyland has a detention area. He referred to it as "Disney Jail."

My son and I attacked him with questions. What did Disney Jail look like? Was it in the back of the Disneyland Police Department on Main Street, U.S.A.? Or was it a separate facility? Was it themed? Was the theme "fantasy jail" like the jail in *The Shawshank Redemption* that all the frat bros love? The highly cinematic jail where you pass over the rape parts and instead get to enjoy male friendships and do male emotional work while hidden away from the terrifying gaze of women, plus all the rock collecting and the movie nights and the cool hole escapes?

Mayor Mark said no. He said Disney Jail is just a locked office. People who sneak in booze and get drunk, or get naked, or shoplift are discreetly brought there to cool off or await the legal punishment of Real-Jail-Land. "It's really nothing special," Mark said.

At this point my son asked, with real curiosity, "Dad, have *you* ever been to Disney Jail?"

"Ha ha," I said. "No."

But then the morning light shifted and the moment became more shadowed.

"Wait," I said. "What do you think is happening when I come out here to LA? Do you think I'm just going to Disneyland all the time? By myself? And then going wild and getting thrown in jail?"

He shrugged. He honestly didn't know.

I told him no, of course not. I would never go to Disneyland alone. And frankly, a middle-aged man in his forties with a beard who is just lurking near the spinning teacups would probably get thrown in Disney Jail long before he had a chance to get drunk and nude in a flying Dumbo. But more, I wouldn't betray him that way.

"I would never go to Disneyland without you," I said. "It would only make me cry."

He accepted this explanation. And throughout the day, Disney Jail offered us a new point of connection. As we walked the park, we considered a thought experiment: if you *had* to get thrown in Disney Jail, what would be the best way to go out?

I suggested that we stand up in the boat in Pirates of the Caribbean and start pointing at the animatronic pirates and villagers, screaming, "These violent delights will have violent ends!"

My son didn't get the *Westworld* reference. Once again, I was reminded that, *Game of Thrones* notwithstanding, HBO only reaches a very small portion of American audiences. That is why I also abandoned the idea of re-creating my most famous scene from *Bored to Death*, riding through the park on a shopping cart tossing chickens at people.

My son suggested playing on sentiment. He recalled that there is a curtained window above the entrance to the Snow White attraction in Fantasyland. Every thirty seconds or so, a robot version of the evil queen Grimhilde (thanks, internet!) parts the curtains to stare down at the crowd for a long beat, before retreating into the darkness and swishing the curtains closed again.

My son suggested going into Fantasyland on his own, crying, claiming to be lost. He would say, "I want my mommy" over and over. Eventually a nice family would come to help him. And then he would say, "Never mind, I found her." He would point up to Grimhilde the evil robot, peering through the curtains. "That is my mommy," he would say, with the flat affect of a child in a horror movie. And then he would call up to her. "I've brought you another family, Mommy," he would say.

As I say, he was nine at the time. I was extremely proud of him for thinking of this and I still am. However, I pointed out, wandering around crying for your mommy is not likely to get you thrown in Disney Jail. It is more likely to have you taken away from us by Disney Child Protective Services—or, for that matter, a murderer.

Finally, we brainstormed two viable options. One was that we would go into the Haunted Mansion and take the Stretching Room down to the hallway that leads to the Doom Buggies.

Ugh. I just realized that you do not live inside my head along with the junkpile of Disneyland backstage lingo that clutters my brain along with all the other junkpile trivia I have in there. To explain: In the Haunted Mansion, there is a spooky hallway you have to walk through before you get strapped into the cars that take you through the ride proper. The spooky hallway is a giddy moment of freedom. After a day of being carefully and psychologically herded from one controlled environment to the next, you almost can't believe that they would just trust you to walk down a hallway. Historically, this has led to some outbursts. It used to be that a cast member would wait here, stiffly, in a suit of armor, and then jump out at guests at random. This practice was discontinued when a woman, already in the full grip of spooky hallway fever, freaked out and punched the cast member in the armored face. But mostly people control themselves and walk through the ride.

My son and I, however, would stop walking. We would quickly take off our clothes, revealing the matching blue satin dresses we wore beneath them. We would put blue bows in our hair and hold each other's hands. "Come play with us," we would tell the passing crowd. "Come play with us forever and ever."

But then I had a better idea. It was better because it would not incriminate my son, who does not deserve a Disney criminal record. And it would also offer an Easter egg to those poor few who were not only aware of my television career, but its trajectory. There is a large, walk-through treehouse in Disneyland. It used to be the Swiss Family Treehouse, but it was re-themed to be Tarzan's Treehouse when that animated movie came out.

To get to the treehouse, you climb a spiral staircase in Adventureland and then walk over a plank bridge. In the middle of the bridge there is nothing: it's just a bridge. But what if, instead of nothing, there was me, wearing only a tangled, matted wig and a loincloth. "Hello," I would say. "Me Tarzan."

Then I would whisper, "Technically, it's me, John Hodgman, playing Tarzan. That is what is happening in my life now. I am known for my nude scenes. Anyway, there's a new rule. It's a Disney rule, not something I just made up. If you want to go in, you have to give me twenty dollars in cash. But if you only have five, that's fine. Really, whatever you can spare. It's not for drugs. It's for my sunstroke fund."

Someday, when I truly have nothing left to lose, I will do this.

Later, as the sun honeyed on the half-empty Mark Twain Riverboat (hint: go on this thing; it's always empty), my family and I drifted past fake shores on a fake river, gliding on rails below the water. But I realized this was real. We were just enjoying each other's company, for once without stress or worry. I don't have to pay money to skip a line for us to be together. We just have to be together. And honestly, the best way to go to Disney Jail? It's to walk up to a family like mine who are cutting the line and spit at them.

When we got off the Mark Twain Riverboat, my son and I saw Mark, the mayor of Frontiertown.

"Look," I said. "It's our friend, the mayor."

He was standing outside the Golden Horseshoe Saloon, handing out flyers and encouraging people to come in and see the show. This seemed beneath the office of mayor of Frontiertown to me, and he seemed tired and dispirited. I knew we would cheer him up.

"Mr. Mayor, Mr. Mayor!" I called out as we walked toward him. But when he saw us, there was a kind of exhausted panic in his eyes. He held his hand out straight and screamed, "No!" Then he pivoted on his booted heel and quick-walked to the saloon's side door. Later Mark would say he just didn't recognize us. It was the end of his shift, and he was tired.

But now we just stood, snubbed, in the middle of Frontiertown. "That's how it goes," I explained to my son. "For a while you're friends with the mayor, and then you're not."

Chapter Eight

SECRET SOCIETY

B y the way, my son was not wrong to suspect me of betraying him. I never did give him that Daredevil car that I bought for him at the airport. When I got on the plane I ran into an acquaintance, a writer who had helped create the *Daredevil* television show. I couldn't resist the chance to show him this hilarious Daredevil car and give it to him. I couldn't resist the chance to make a television person smile by giving him my son's present. Nor was my son wrong to suspect that I might be going crazy while out of his sight.

Some months earlier, I had gone back to Yale, my alma mater, and given some advice to young people. Don't worry, I was invited. It has not gotten to the point yet that I am just taking the train up there randomly to rant at college students (although that feels inevitable). Mainly the advice I gave the young people was, don't get drunk and fall down the stairs.

You may recall from my last book that Yale has a number of secret societies: invitation-only clubs for seniors that conspire within large, windowless clubhouses called "tombs." You may also recall that when I was a freshman I was invited to a party at one particular secret society called Book and Snake. Personally, I barely recall this. I got so excited to be going to the party that, when I got there, I got drunk and fell down the stairs. I hit my head and woke up in the emergency room, and when I did, my memories of the secret society had been erased forever.

That was a funny story until I had children. It takes a long time for white guys to appreciate that they are breakable. They do not live from birth with the daily fear that they might be attacked or detained or killed. Their bodies are not constant targets of power. Their bodies *are* power, so they throw those bodies up and down mountains and stairs and out of airplanes and into pointless online yelling matches for fun. They just presume they will survive. I see these guys every morning when I am driving my son to school. Many people who ride in the new bike lanes in New York City are cautious and considerate. They take the responsibility of their newly authorized right of way seriously, stopping at red lights, signaling turns, remembering that I am driving many hundreds of pounds of unstoppable steel momentum and they are riding on top of a delicate steampunk emulation of a greyhound.

But there are always a few each morning who zip the wrong way down the one-way street, weave through the closing narrow spaces between you and that moving bus, then slap the roof of your car in anger. They are always white dudes. They are usually wearing jean jackets, almost never have helmets, and frequently have young children loosely strapped onto the backs of their bikes. Their children are protected, of course, by bicycle righteousness and white dude force field. I look forward to them yelling at me on Twitter.

My body had grown creaky and fragile and I had learned through sad experience that not even cars, never mind jean jackets and sanctimony, protect us from tragic outcomes. I could have died in that secret society, as my own parents told me at the time. And even though I didn't, it seems a reckless story to tell your children, who look to you to learn how to live in the world. Still, I told them all about it. I only have so much material.

We had all gone up to New Haven for my twentieth college reunion, and the first thing I noticed was that everyone had gotten much older except me. It was very mysterious. With the exception of me, everyone was all paunchy and puffy-faced and suit-wearing, all weird moms and sad dads.

Aging shows first in the eyes. The eyes of your friends droop and crinkle at the corners, they glaze a bit and darken, and they don't like what they are seeing because what they are seeing is you. They see you at their college reunion and say to themselves, *If he looks like* that, *what do* I *look like? I've been living with my own face all this time, so I haven't noticed it change. But now I see John Hodgman, and I worry, am* I *also aging? Have I changed and gnarled and crinkled and puffed as much as he has? Do I also have a terrible beard I haven't noticed?*

I saw one old classmate who had always been so handsome. He had looked like a J.Crew model, and I am talking back in the 1990s, when looking like a J.Crewman *mattered*, so let's call him Bob Barnjacket. He was still very handsome, but his cheeks were a little sunken now, his eyes tired in their sockets. He had just the slightest air of jaunty cadaver about him that you see in some veteran game show hosts.

But even though we were all horrifying reminders of our own mortality, it was nice to see my old, crumbling friends. The rain was apocalyptic, and we gathered under the tent in our summerweight suits and dresses and drank our gins and wines and told our stories, like *The Canterbury Tales* directed by Wes Anderson.

If you're wondering, Nicholas still wears bright orange shirts, and Adam is writing for TV now. Andrea moved to Alaska years ago to practice law. She and her Alaskan husband are thinking of moving to Hawaii. They are only interested in the extremes. Hugo is still working on documentaries and was rocking a crushed-velvet blazer the color of reddest wine with cream-colored piping on the lapels.

"You know I like piping," Hugo said.

I knew.

That easy-smiling guy whose Walkman I always used to borrow without asking still held no grudge against me. He had been just this happy and confident when he was a teenager. Partly it was just his disposition, but also, I think, it came from his calming knowledge, marrow-deep, that he would always be protected by his family's generations of wealth. I remember pondering at the time what it would be like to never have to work a day in your life. I would tell myself I was disgusted by this concept, but in fact I was jealous, because I am lazy. He wasn't. He was diligent and friendly and generous. Now he was a doctor, the kind who directly saves a lot of lives. His eyes were placid and kind, and I won't say more about him because I don't want him to know that he still makes me feel small and covetous.

Then there was the woman who had been an actor for a while, and then became a single mother, but now is trying to write and record children's music and also work in textiles. She had a bright and terrified light in her eyes. I barely knew her in college, but I felt very close to her now. She didn't know if any of her decisions had been good so far, and she doubted that any she made from here on would work, but she didn't know what else to do. She had to keep going.

It occurred to me that the happy, unhaunted people I met at the reunion had finished their journeys long ago, maybe as early as age eighteen. They still had school to attend and papers to write, yes, but even as fresh-persons they were already whole and happy for some damn reason. Others travel deep into their forties and still never arrive at the calm that lurked in Dr. Lifesaver's eyes. Even if they are successful, something is missing, some calling or breakthrough or validation that always feels out of reach, like a chunk of lost time in a windowless tomb.

I explained this to my children as we walked around the next day. We had come across Book and Snake, the secret society where I had fallen down the stairs, the tomb that might have been my own. I told them how haunted I had always been by the fact that my body had gone on a journey that my brain could not recall. And that's when I noticed: the door was open. It was just casually ajar, like it was someone's unattended back porch and not a two-story limestone vault. It had been almost twenty-five years. "I want to go in," I told my children. I wanted to see what I had seen.

I tiptoed across the street and up to the door. My children tiptoed behind me. It was broad daylight, but we were stealthy. Once we reached the door, I could see warm yellow light in a marble lobby. I did not hear any voices. I put my camera phone gently into the breach and took a picture. Later I would see that I had taken a photo of a bell, engraved and heavy, mounted in a pale niche in the entrance chamber. It was a blurry shot, because my hand had jumped back when one of the children started knocking loudly on the door.

"No, no, no!" I yelled. But they didn't understand. They had been taught to be honest and forthright and not sneak around and take creepshots of bells. I turned and was prepared to make . . . not a run-for-it exactly, but an overcasual-fast-walk-for-it to escape when I heard my name.

"John?" I heard. I turned around. It was Bob Barnjacket. He was inside the tomb, opening the door, confused. He was a Book and Snake alum, it turned out. I had never known he was a member. If I had, maybe I would have tried to be better friends. Maybe I could have used that friendship to get back into that tomb *years* ago. (I am a great person with good values.) But now he was opening the door. He was wearing street clothes. Not robes or a creepy mask or anything.

"What are you doing?" he asked.

I apologized. I explained to him about how I had fallen down the stairs, and how I had always wanted to go back inside. He opened the door a little wider.

"Oh," he said. "It's really not a big deal. We were just finishing an alumni brunch. Do you want to come inside, right now?"

I don't know how to describe the feeling I had in that moment. The symbol of this secret society is the *ouroboros*, a snake eating its own tail, an emblem of recurrence and eternity. Life does not offer many perfect circles, and now I was about to complete mine. Or eat my own butt like the stupidest snake in the world. The visual language of the *ouroboros* can be read either way.

But just as I was about to cross the threshold, a trim, older woman in a yellow sweater came from around the back of the door and held her hand up. She said, simply, "No, no, no."

Later I would learn her name was Nancy. She was an older alumna of the tomb and, today, its appointed guardian.

"No?" Bob said to her.

"No, no, no," she said.

"Sorry," Bob said. Nancy closed the door on me.

I explained to my children that it was a fitting ending. Some mysteries are designed to remain.

And that was the end of the story, until the following October, when I received an email. Two current members of Book and Snake, a young man and a young woman, had heard my story. They were sorry I had been turned away, and invited me to the tomb for dinner with the current class of secret people. I won't reveal the names of the young man and woman. Let's call them Booker and Snakea.

I obviously said yes, and after some back-and-forth on dates, I went up to New Haven on a Thursday to have a secret dinner.

I arrived at the familiar door, and this time it was opened wide for me. *Finally*, I thought. Here was the little marble entrance chamber and the bell I had taken that creepshot of. This much was familiar. I wish I could say that as I wandered through those secret chambers, the memory came flooding back to me, but it didn't. Not even the stairs looked familiar, which is strange, since I had such a close relationship with them, and honestly most staircases look pretty much the same. I had pictured a grand, open staircase with a regal red carpet, but this was just a dark, enclosed stairwell, twisting up like a snake through cramped and windowless dark until it reached the main meeting chamber. This room had a tall and vaulted ceiling that was painted with clouds. I stared into those clouds but they formed no shapes that I recognized. Whatever secret knowledge I hoped I would remember here was gone forever.

Instead, I just had dinner with sixteen very nice young people, plus a pleasant older man with snowy white hair. He was introduced as an alum, who, like the woman who had shushed me out the door, was there to serve as the wary grown-up, lest too many secrets be spilled. There were also a couple of more recent alums, including a man named Doug who, at thirty-one, had just been named the transportation tsar of New Haven. If you are a fan of Alex Jones and were worried that the bus schedules and traffic routing of some southern Connecticut cities are under the control of Ivy League secret societies, I am here to tell you: that is absolutely correct.

Here are the secrets of the secret society dinner: The dining room is in the lowest level of the tomb. It's long and oval and comfortable, with wood paneling and red leather chairs. The chairs feature the *ouroboros* I mentioned, death and rebirth emblazoned on every seat back. Wine and beer are served, but no hard alcohol. Your entrée choices are swordfish and veal, served by a local caterer, who is presumably not killed or blinded at the end of every dinner, but probably has mixed feelings about serving secret dinners to children every Thursday. If you show up ten minutes late, all the spanakopita will be gone.

And of course there are no windows. If you have ever dreamed of dining in a luxury survival bunker with a group of luminous young people who have been selected by a committee to preserve the species, dinner at Book and Snake will make your dream come true.

We had a nice time. The young people asked me how I came to be successful. I told them my answer. I told them that the secret to my implausible, financially self-sufficient adulthood was the same secret that had brought me here: I was invited to do something, and I said yes.

It is better to say yes than no. Unless saying yes will hurt you or someone else, say yes. Don't say no if the invitation is scary. That's when you should definitely say yes. If a computer company invites you to be in an ad and you're scared to say yes because (a) it will mess up your pickup schedule at your child's school and (b) it will push you well past your comfortable limits of fraudulency and change your life forever, take it from me, don't say no, like I did, and then get lucky only because they asked again. They won't always ask again. And don't say no, like I did, to appearing on *Breaking Bad* because you were afraid to live in Albuquerque for a while, away from your family. Do your work. Do the things you love. Don't ask permission. The more work you make in the world, the more likely someone will ask you to do some new thing, some bigger thing, or at least some interesting thing. And when they ask, say yes.

I didn't tell them then to not get drunk and fall down the stairs. Not yet. Not in front of the grown-up.

At the end of dinner, the grown-up man led the secret societians in a song that I found adorable, but they seemed a little embarrassed by. But then the grown-up man left and the secret societians brought me to the cozy room. There they put on Otis Redding's "(Sittin' On) The Dock of the Bay," and they didn't seem embarrassed by *that* at all, so who knows about young people and music these days.

The cozy room was on the ground floor, right off the bell chamber: a purgatory between the airy upstairs clouds and the red leather dining bunker below. Here are the secrets of this room: It looked like a college dorm. There were big sofas with blankets draped over them. Amid the photos of past classes of secret societans and a wooden plaque hung with ceremonial tankards were bookshelves stacked with DVDs of *The Shining* and *The O.C.* A bunch of spooky blank face masks, part of some ritual maybe, were dumped without ceremony in a pile on the shelf. Another shelf was dedicated to Bananagrams and spent Nerf darts. My normal loathing of Bananagrams was quelled by the charming dumpiness of the whole experience. The bathroom toilet paper roll was empty. Get it together, Illuminati.

We settled into the deep, ratty chairs and they opened the lid on a hinged wooden captain's chest tucked into the corner. I don't like to narc on these kids, but can you guess what was in it? Of course it was alcohol: a small cache of hard liquor they kept hidden from their nightly grown-up and only brought out after he left. Secrets within secrets, and I was of their society. They offered me a drink from their motley, college-y stock: there was gold rum and silver rum and, weirdly, a bottle of Fernet-Branca. It was like they grabbed what they could from a Sky Lounge and ran.

I should have had the Fernet-Branca. That's a weird drink for a weird old man who doesn't know to leave the secret clubhouse after the ritual song and let the young people be. But I didn't. I took their rum and listened to their secrets.

One handsome white guy who had skipped dinner flopped down on the couch and told me he thought college only brainwashed you into wanting to make money. He told me he was really only good at rolling blunts and shooting three-pointers.

But he didn't want to play basketball anymore, and he had no plans after graduation. He had a one-way ticket to Hawaii and was just going to see what happened. I tried to hate him, but I couldn't.

Another young man who had not skipped dinner and was wearing a nice jacket and tie told me he wanted to go into the legal cannabis industry. I am certain he is a billionaire now. Cornelius Vanderbilt II made his fortune in trains. His son was to attend Yale, but died of typhoid fever first, so Vanderbilt funded a gothic dormitory in his memory, featuring one particularly luxurious apartment with chandeliers and marble fireplaces where his dead son would never live. I had no difficulty imagining that the future held a hall or a library or an edibles research center on campus paid for by the fortune of this soon-to-be pot baron.

Maybe Pot Baron would name it after his old beautiful Stoner Athlete friend who had taken a one-way trip to Hawaii to throw his body and privilege away and snapped his neck in a cliff-diving accident in Oahu. Just kidding. Probably Pot Baron would hire Stoner Athlete as a brand ambassador, a handsome man just rolling blunts and shooting three-pointers on sponsored social media, and they both would be happy and wealthy forever.

Booker and Snakea, my hosts, were also hanging around. We talked a little about my last visit to the tomb, and Booker asked if they could officially call the act of falling down the stairs "pulling a Hodgman." I told them yes, but it would cost them a lot of money.

"But seriously," I said, "don't get drunk and fall down the

stairs." Philip Seymour Hoffman had just died of a drug overdose, and what I needed to say was: Don't kill yourself. Yes, take risks, but if you can help it, don't do dumb things for no reason. Try not to black out, try not to kill yourself on purpose or by accident, or to succumb to the slow darkening death of addiction. Whether you get drunk and hit your head or just stop paying attention, don't let your body stray in the world while you are absent. Years and whole lives are lost that way, so easily. Stick around if you can help it.

It was an awkward thing to say, surrounded by young people drinking their rum.

"Just be responsible," I said, "and stick to growing and selling marijuana."

Snakea tried to change the subject. "Maybe we should play a game," she said.

And Pot Baron said, "What about Fantasy?"

I guess this is a parlor game of some kind, but I am still not sure. I have tried to search for the rules, but "Fantasy" is an unspecific and, depending on your content filters, provocative thing to type into a search engine. If you know the rules, reader, let me know sometime. But I did not want to let these children know any of my fantasies (in part because I was living one of them), so I said, "No thank you."

Then Snakea asked, "Why don't you tell us your deepest fear?"

Whatever Fantasy was, this was worse. I had not written my last book yet then, so they could not know that I had already conquered most of my old fears: of going to the dump, of being unliked by even one single person on earth, of being naked, ever. But these had been replaced by new fears—such as losing a child—and even more terrifying certainties, like the slow 2 a.m. horror that pushes the breath out of your body when you realize you are only five years younger than your mother was when she died. These are the fears you keep secret from young people. They will know them eventually anyway, so why ruin the surprise?

So I cheated. I didn't tell them my deepest fear, but instead my greatest phobia, which is, of course, underwater robots.

You are young people, I explained, so you probably never had a chance to ride the 20,000 Leagues Under the Sea attraction in the Magic Kingdom at Walt Disney World. But I had gone there when I was in high school. I was on a school trip with the high school chorus. We were on tour performing selections from the year's musical, *The Pirates of Penzance*, and because Rob Crawford was touring colleges and couldn't go with us, I had been promoted from "Pirate" to "Pirate King." I am forever failing upward.

Our tour consisted of exactly two stops: an Orlando-area high school and a lame Disney World–adjacent pavilion next to a man-made lake, where we sang for about nine elderly people. The rest of the time, we had the run of the park.

I chose to go on the fake submarine ride based on the movie *20,000 Leagues Under the Sea* because there was no line. When I got into the fake submarine and peered out beneath the surface of the water, I presumed I was going to see real fish that had been trapped in this fake lagoon. However, I learned it was worse than I imagined. There were no real fish in that fake lagoon, only fake fish, and worse, fake fish that *moved*, and even double worse, fake mermaids and fake giant clams and one giant fake squid that also moved, because they were robots. Robots underwater.

This should not be, I told the members of the secret society. It was not just the fear of electrocution that gripped me, but an existential nausea deeper than any uncanny valley, and one I cannot completely articulate today. All the time that I had been walking around the park, in the sun of the surface world, I had no idea that here, beneath this dark and oily water, robots were moving, constantly gazing blindly into the murk, flapping their tails and waving their tentacles. Even as I write this, my skin prickles on my forearms, and it feels like even my hands want to vomit.

And this is not the worst part, I told my fellow secreteers. The worst part was that about five years after I rode it, the 20,000 Leagues Under the Sea attraction closed. I guess the national mania for James Mason movies from the '60s had finally come to an end. But rather than saying "good riddance" and covering that nightmare hole with Chernobyl levels of concrete, Disney kept the lagoon full, of both water and robots, for ten years. Ten *years*.

"It was ten years," I said, "before they finally drained that lagoon and took the robots out. And for all of those ten years, they waited there, those robo-mermaids and squids and clams and turtles and fish, still and unmoving in fetid water that was no longer even churned by the occasional fake submarine. And if you were to get drunk, say, and fall down the stairs, or even just slip over a fake wooden handrail and plunge into that oily pool, your feet might... touch them."

This was not a metaphor for anything, I explained to my new young friends. I was just telling them the truth. When I watch old YouTube videos of the ride today, my heart races. And even now, long after the attraction has been replaced with a *Finding Nemo* ride, even here in a safe, windowless limestone fortress in New Haven, I was still worried that I might slip off the couch and fall into that awful water, and my heart beat hard.

They took this in. And then Booker said (and this is true!), "I don't believe you. I don't believe any of what you just said. You're just playing Fantasy right now."

"How?" I said. "I DO NOT EVEN KNOW WHAT THAT GAME IS!"

"You know what?" said not Snakea, but a different young woman. "You remind me of Will Shortz."

And I said, "That is the meanest thing a twenty-two-year-old woman could ever say to me."

She said, "No! Will Shortz is a complicated guy!" which did not make me feel better and cannot actually be true. Can it?

Booker finally said he believed me. And then he asked: "Do you want to become an honorary member of our Secret Society?"

This was a hard question to answer. I had never really sought membership in any club or society when I was in college. Even then I mostly just wanted to see the inside of the secret house, and I had gotten that. Also, I never wanted to *ask*. I was the anti-Groucho in this regard. I never wanted to belong to a club that didn't already want me as a member. They should have to want me so badly that they would just let me in without my having to work for it.

And now that was happening. I wanted to say yes yes yes. Because we were all friends, hanging out together. All night I kept expecting to realize that I was not twenty-two anymore. But it didn't happen! I had not lost a step. We were joking and laughing and drinking and listening to Otis Redding and they did not want me to leave, they wanted me to stay. I could be twenty-two again, and forever. And that's the most dangerous game of Fantasy of all.

That is what Nancy who lives behind the door knew. This is why she said, *No, no, no. This is not for you! We are not insured for you. You are in your forties, and if you fell down the stairs tonight it would have a different meaning, and not be so quickly forgotten. This tomb was never yours, and you cannot have it. Go find your own.*

I am glad to say that I received her message at last. "No thank you," I said. "But thank you." We took some pictures together, wearing dark robes, and then I walked back to my grown-up hotel room and went to bed. I did not fall down the stairs, but one young man pretended to so I could take his picture. He was pulling a Hodgman, and my legacy lives on.

Chapter Nine

CAREER ADVICE
FOR CHILDREN

I do not merely have incredibly good advice for college students. That is why this chapter is specifically for the weird, precocious thirteen-year-olds who are reading this book. I know you are out there. Over the many book tours and shows I have done, I have met you in the signing lines, accompanied by your patient and enabling parents and guardians. You are all beautiful oddballs with glasses and interesting haircuts and hobbies and journals. I like you, and I'm sorry for all the swear words in this book so far. I suspect that you like me because you recognize in me the very weird, very precocious thirteen-year-old I once was. But the truth is, that is long behind me. I am almost fifty, and I have had a lot of experiences in a lot of jobs.

I have been, in my life, a professional writer, actor, comedian, food columnist, literary agent, receptionist, cheesemonger, telemarketer, dishwasher, popcorn seller, video store clerk (that's something you only see at the Renaissance faire anymore), soup ladler, traffic counter, stockroom attendant,

English-muffin-pizza salesperson, and now, the author of this book.

I started working when I was a little older than you. I didn't have to go to work. Both my parents had good jobs. But it never occurred to me not to. To me, work meant meeting other humans and learning about them. Sometimes it meant getting paid, but not always. The important thing was that I got to pretend I was a grown-up, which is the dream of every only child.

(I am still pretending to be a grown-up, by the way. That's a job that never ends.)

I have learned a lot from all my jobs—it's not all just "say yes" and "don't get drunk and fall down the stairs." I would like to share these lessons with my own children, but they are not interested in me at all. That's OK. That's *their* job. So since you are here anyway, I'm going to give you some career advice, and I'm not going to sugarcoat it. I mean, among other things, I will talk about pornography. But you can handle it. Because you're smart.

ENGLISH-MUFFIN-PIZZA SALES

When I was your age, I was pretty much a genius. I didn't invent the English muffin pizza. I read about it on the back of a jar of tomato sauce. But I *was* the one who decided to make them and sell them out of a window of my house.

It was a great business plan. After all, we had a whole box of English muffins and a bunch of shredded cheese just sitting there in the refrigerator. I was already holding the jar of sauce in my hand. I wouldn't have to pay rent, and I would refuse to pay taxes. It was going to be pure profit.

I presented this idea to Peter, my friend who lived next door, and we agreed to be partners. I liked him. He was a couple of years older than me and so he lent the business an air of maturity. As well, the bay window in my mother's office, which was to be our storefront, opened onto an attractive patio (with seating). This was very nice, but the patio was hidden on three sides by huge rhododendrons. Foot traffic would be a problem, so I knew we were going to have to rely on advertising, and Peter would help spread the word. We split up the neighborhood and covered it with photocopied flyers announcing that two children were selling English muffin pizzas for a quarter, and that people were invited to trespass onto my parents yard to get them.

My parents had paid for the flyers. They also paid for the additional English muffins, cheese, and jars of sauce that we stocked up on. They may have called it a "budget" or a "loan." But they paid.

We opened on a Saturday. I think we were wise enough not to make too many English muffin pizzas in advance. We sold maybe nine. Some of our customers were kids, but mostly they were adults. They were all neighbors and friends of our parents, and they all just *happened* to be wanting an English muffin pizza in the middle of a humid spring afternoon, and luckily here we were, selling them! This puzzled me at first, but gradually I put it together: they were liars (not even *good* liars) who had been sent in by our parents. And that is what soured me on the English-muffin-pizza biz forever. It was how I learned that there is such a thing as a dishonest day's work.

Look, absolutely start a lemonade stand. It gets you out on the street and talking to people. If you're lucky, and you live in Park Slope like I do, maybe Vincent D'Onofrio will come around and not buy anything and just smoke a cigarette and stare at you. That's cool. That's Vincent D'Onofrio's job. And sure, let your parents pay for the lemonade. You'll get a story out of it.

But don't let somebody set you up in a cushy fake job in your mom's office. Don't let your parents send shills in to buy your pizza muffins out of pity or obligation. This is good advice even if you're not thirteen, because there are more of these kinds of jobs than you think.

TRENCH DIGGER

My first job with a real boss was working with Tim McGonagle's grown-up cousin. He was a contractor and he hired us to dig trenches around a house he was working on. It was summertime, and it was hot work. As we dug the trenches, Tim's cousin laid down PVC pipe. The pipe had holes punched along the side. I remember thinking, *That pipe is all broken. How will that work?* I knew nothing about drainage then. That is how young I was.

We broke for lunch and we ate our huge Italian subs and heaping handfuls of Planters cheese balls. Tim's grown-up cousin brought out a two-liter plastic bottle of iced coffee. "I make the best iced coffee," he said. "A ton of milk, a ton of sugar. It tastes like coffee ice cream." It really did. He poured it around and we poured it on top of our subs and cheese balls and laughed in the shade. We drank a lot of it, even though we had a lot more work to do in that hot sun.

You might think, *I know where this story is going. You ended up vomiting all those meats and balls and milky coffee right into the trench and all those clean new mysterious pipe holes. And then Tim's cousin made you clean your vomit up with a hose.*

Nope. None of that happened. We just had a delicious lunch and did not throw up because we were fourteen and could eat like monsters. The point of the story is that Tim's cousin brought coffee for everyone, which is how to be a great boss, and also that your lunch break, especially after shared hard physical work, is amazing. You should enjoy it, and then you should eat whatever you want because you're young.

But yes, when you hit your thirties (twenties, if you're working at a desk), don't shove a huge double cheeseburger and a milk shake in your face on your lunch break every day. You don't want to feel sick and sleepy for the rest of the day. Just have a light lunch. Don't eat like a child if you aren't one.

STOCKROOM CLERK

I earned my first printed paycheck working in a stockroom. The stockroom was on the top floor of a squat and beautiful gothic building off Newbury Street in Boston. The other floors housed a European furniture company that my mom liked. Before that it had been an art house movie theater, and before that it had been built as a spiritualist temple. After that it became a bookstore, and now I think it is a school. It didn't matter to me. I was sorry to have missed the movie theater, but I would have worked in any of those businesses. I liked the neighborhood, and I liked the building, and I liked walking up to it. That is maybe the most important thing about any job.

One-half of my job was to take calls from the sales floor. They would give me a SKU number for a piece of furniture they had sold. I would have to find the flat-pack box that matched the number, put it on a dolly, and bring it down in the freight elevator for the customer. Sometimes the customer would ask me to tie the flat-pack box of European furniture to the roof of his car. I would do this with a big box of twine. I felt I got to be pretty good at tying those boxes on, but how do I know? Maybe half of them flew off the car on Route 9. Maybe I accidentally caused accidents and killed a bunch of people. I hope not. One time a young dad tipped me a couple of dollars after I tied a box to his car, and I have never, ever forgotten it. I can picture him right now, and consider him a hero of this universe. Tipping may seem cold and transactional, but in fact it makes everyone feel more human. So don't be a cheapskate.

The other half of my job was to unload trucks. Two or three mornings a week a huge semitrailer would angle itself impossibly into the alleyway next to the former spiritualist temple.

The truck was full of wooden pallets of shrink-wrapped flat-packs and foam loveseats and torchieres. We would bring the pallets up in the freight elevator, one by one.

There were a number of different truck drivers, both men and women, as well as one husband-and-wife team. Mostly they were lonely men who had been driving all night long. Sometimes the truck driver would just go to sleep in his or her cab while we worked. Sometimes they just needed some human contact first. When they wanted to chat, my manager, who had a degree in third-wave jazz trumpet from the New England Conservatory of Music, would send me to buy coffee for the truck driver and the rest of us. Again: a good boss.

One summer morning, we were having coffee on the loading dock with a truck driver named Dominic. Dominic said he had been on the road for a week, away from his wife and son. But he had a small TV and VCR in his cab. He told us about the movies he watched.

"Last night, I saw a movie called *Ladyhawke*," he said. He gave us a whole rundown. It was a fantasy film in which Rutger Hauer and Michelle Pfeiffer played cursed lovers. Rutger Hauer turns into a wolf by night. Michelle Pfeiffer turns into a hawk by day. They travel together. But only briefly, at dawn and twilight, can they see each other in their true human forms, and then the moment is gone.

I don't remember Rutger Hauer's character's name, but I do know the woman was named Isabeau. I remember because Dominic really liked it.

"The woman's name is Isabeau," said Dominic. "Isn't that a beautiful name?"

I knew about *Ladyhawke*, of course. I was aware of all the fantasy and science fiction movies that were being released, but I had passed on seeing this one. It seemed derivative and slight to a hateful, sixteen-year-old me. That said, it was *definitely* in my wheelhouse, and I was startled when Dominic mentioned it. It was the first time I considered that a long-haul truck driver and I might watch the same kind of movie.

I felt immediate shame. Though my parents had raised me in an affluent suburb of Boston, my mom and dad both came from working-class families. Not truck drivers specifically, but people who worked in factories and printing presses and kept house. My grandparents and aunts and uncles liked hockey and beer and the Village People and didn't for a second think the Village People were gay. And they loved me, even though I was a long-haired weirdo whose belly chub was packed into a *Bloom County* T-shirt and who felt out of place in their tidy, small homes, homes that didn't sit on prosperous leafy streets or have so many extra rooms that I could claim one just to practice the clarinet in. I loved them back, except for my one cousin who pulled a hank of my hair out in front of me and set it on fire, laughing. But even though I had been raised in a liberal town and steeped in public television open-mindedness, I realized now on the loading dock that I was a snob.

Of course my aunts and uncles and grandparents knew the Village People were gay. They weren't dumb. And of course fantasy and science fiction is not reserved only for weird suburban white nerds like me (though they are fighting hard now to keep it for themselves). Fantasy and science fiction is also for grown-up truck drivers who miss their families and dream about the morning they will be reunited with them, however briefly. Then they can forget *this* morning, having coffee with the failed jazz musician and the teenage snob with the Keith Haring Swatch.

My dawning class awareness was nothing to brag about. It's just to say that work makes your world bigger and shows you your mistakes. It helps you to see other people in their human forms.

"Isn't Isabeau a beautiful name?" Dominic said. And even though I had enough high school French to know that, even in a made-up fantasy world, ending a woman's name with the masculine *beau* made no sense, I had to agree that it was.

MOVIE THEATER EMPLOYEE

Toward the end of high school, I worked several summers in a beautiful old movie theater. It was the best job I ever had.

The movie theater had once shown old black-and-white movies, and I would go to it frequently. But by the time I was seventeen, when I started working there, it was a second-run house. That meant it showed movies that had already had a full run somewhere else. Nobody wanted to see *Who Framed Roger Rabbit* a year after its first run, so we were not very busy.

My manager at the movie theater was a man named Harry. The projectionist was also named Harry. They were friends and both in their thirties, I guess. They just felt like grown-ups to me. The first Harry was a huge, heavy man whose voice boomed and laughed. He was like a very handsome full-size Muppet who had trained as a fine arts painter. The second Harry was normal-sized and also an artist, making sculptures out of neon tubes. He was more quietly mischievous. If First Harry was Sweetums, Second Harry was more of a Salacious Crumb. They both needed day jobs, but the movie theater wasn't it. First Harry painted houses and eventually went to work for the Commonwealth of Massachusetts. Second Harry was an engineer at Bose. They worked at the movie theater because they liked each other and the other coworkers and it was fun.

Work was easy. After the nine people who had bought tickets to the movie had gone in, we didn't have much to do. If it was not too hot out, we would haul the blue bench out and sit on it and make jokes.

If you can work in a beautiful old movie theater, especially if it's one you used to go to as a kid, you should do it. Here are some of the good feelings:

- Walking behind the concession stand and no one yelling at you
- Walking into the theater to watch ten minutes of a movie without paying and then walking out knowing

you can just finish it tomorrow (also without anyone
yelling at you)
- Being locked into a box office and organizing the cash
into neat stacks, all facing the same way, and being
trusted to do this
- Going with ticket stubs to get discounts at the ice cream
place and the bookstore across the street, and also offering free movies to their employees, because you are
all part of a retail secret society
- Sitting on a bench and telling a joke to one of the Harrys and making him laugh

It was a profound sense of belonging. Walking into work felt
like coming home, but a home filled with a family that was
more fun and interesting than my own. I am an only child, and
I thought I was happy that way. But the Harrys were my older
brothers. Second Harry introduced me to Moxie and taught me
to dip french fries into the popcorn butter and to hold the cup
well below the coffee spigot so that it aerates, which was bullshit but it looked cool.

First Harry hired me to help scrape some windows and
taught me that there are no stupid questions, only fuck-ups.
And I'm sorry to swear, but he taught me there is decency in
crudeness when it is blunt and honest. He made the funniest
dirty joke I had ever heard, and even though I later put it together that he borrowed it from the Firesign Theatre, only he

would think to link it to the Louis Malle film *Le Souffle au Coeur*, and it reshaped my brain.

I had had older brothers before, older dude friends who were wilder and riskier than me. I loved them and love them still, but I had a real type. It took me a while to appreciate that they were all alcoholics. The Harrys weren't. Well, actually, First Harry was a *recovered* alcoholic. He was the one who taught me that you can be friends with addicts, and even love them, but you have to know they cannot completely love you back. I don't mean he showed this to me: he sat me down and talked to me about it bluntly, and I'm still grateful.

Their trust in me made me bold and unanxious. I felt so comfortable at the movie theater that, as part of some elaborate joke one night, I went out and lay down in the middle of the street. I was never in danger. Cars moved around me without complaint. I could feel Coolidge Corner, my whole universe, gently surround me and make safe room for me. I could hear the Harrys laughing.

(But you shouldn't do this. Not just because it was dangerous and maybe led to me feeling it was OK to get drunk and fall down the stairs, but because it was worse: it was inconsiderate. People just trying to drive home and get on with their lives shouldn't have to deal with you lying in the street having a life moment.)

I had other work siblings, too, some who were my age. And there were crushes and inspirations and nemeses on staff. It was a whole sitcom. There was even a local cabbie who dropped by as a recurring character and a grumpy janitor who literally lived in the basement. I never wanted to leave, and happily worked on Christmas Eve. Christmas was an easy shift, plus time and a half, and I wanted to be with my family.

But work families do not last. The younger ones of us drifted off to other cities for college or other schemes. The older ones, the ones who had already gone to college (or at least to art school) woke up one day and said, "This isn't a family. I am just working in a movie theater," and left one by one. Also, selling nine tickets a day to a movie was no way to run a business, and eventually the movie theater closed. Don't worry. It opened again: a local community nonprofit bought it and it is thriving. You can still see Second Harry's neon sculpture above the concession stand. But you won't find the bench. On the last night of its original incarnation, after we all said good-bye, I stole it. I carried it home on my shoulders, in part because I wanted to impress my older brothers with one last bit of mischief. In part because I never wanted to forget it.

I don't know where the bench is now.

TRAFFIC COUNTER

I mentioned in my previous book that I worked as a traffic counter when I was in college. I would get up before dawn and go to an assigned street corner. I had a clipboard with a series of counters on it, and I would count the number of cars that turned left, and the number that turned right, and the number that went straight.

I had no idea why I was doing this. Sometimes I wondered if it was all a Yale Psychology Department experiment to see how long they could trick a student into standing by himself on a corner, counting meaningless things, and writing those numbers down on a sheet of paper that would never be read, but simply thrown into a trash can full of fire in some graduate student's cubicle. I wondered if they were watching me from some nearby window, if they were waiting for me to figure out that the job was stupid, to give up and go back to bed, warm and refreshed and untricked, just like every other test subject had done after a single pointless morning of clicking clickers in the cold. But they didn't know who they were dealing with. They didn't know that when you give John Hodgman rules, he follows them all the way, day after shivering day. This is not a virtue. There is the slimmest line between doing a good job for its own sake and following orders to your own frozen death (or someone else's).

You are lucky if you don't know how cold you get when you are in the predawn October darkness, sitting on a low concrete wall by the side of the road. You are lucky if you do not know how much the sun, even the low, pale sun of October, warms you when it arrives, how you wait for it to touch the outer layer of your four jackets and three pairs of pants, and how even those extra few degrees burn away despair. Actually, you are unlucky if you do *not* know this. It's important to know what it's like to be without actual shelter, first of all. And more metaphorically, it's good to know how easy it is to forget, when you're suffering, that the sun is still coming, and it is still warm.

Anyway, I had to wear a bunch of pants to keep warm.

What I didn't mention in my last book was that the job paid $12.50 an hour. This was real money. Roughly $3,000 an hour in 1989 dollars. Or it felt that way. I had very few expenses. I could rent movies for two dollars. Comic books only cost seventy-five cents, and I won't tell you what whiskey cost then because you are a child. For a while, I lived the high life. For a while, I thought, *Maybe I should do this forever.*

In the end, I am glad I didn't become a professional traffic counter and instead finished college. It eventually allowed me to get a job that paid less (working in book publishing), but at least I knew *why* I was doing it, and I only had to wear one pair of pants. Later, as an actor, as you have learned, I sometimes got to wear no pants at all. That's nice work if you can get it.

CHEESE SHOP EMPLOYEE

I also mentioned in my previous book that I worked for a while in a cheese shop. I won't repeat myself, but if you ever find yourself at age nineteen working in a cheese shop in London, there are a few things you should know.

First, it will be the best job you ever had. Your responsibilities will be limited to cutting and tasting fancy cheese and talking to the wealthy weirdos who can afford it. One of these might be an elegant, funny woman who asks you to recommend the strongest possible cheese because she has no sense of smell. She lost it after she was randomly attacked by a lunatic while lying out in the sun on a luxury cruise ship. You will recommend Roquefort and she will smile charitably, because it really was the most obvious choice. But at least it is not Stilton. Stilton is chump cheese.

Another might be the longtime percussionist for Elton John, famed for his live seven-minute solos on the congas and the gong, who might arrive at any moment in his stormcloud-gray Bentley to collect two loaves of ciabatta and pay for them with a check from Coutts, the fanciest bank in all of England, filling it out in perfect copperplate, taking about a week to complete the final flourish on his elaborate signature. You will never forget this.

But mostly you will just be standing, doing nothing, in a room full of good smells. And by the way, Stilton is absolutely *not* chump cheese. It's a noble cheese, though a little boring as a go-to. "Stilton is chump cheese" is just something you will say one morning as you rise up out of some cheese dream. Yes, you will dream about cheese, and it will be the only time you dream about your work and enjoy it.

But, here is this warning. If there is a stereo in the cheese store, you may be tempted to put on the album *Swordfishtrombones* by your very favorite, Mr. Tom Waits. And then it's *possible* that when you do, a beautiful woman might come in. She will buy some cheese, and then make a lot of eye contact with you. And she will say, "What is this music?"

And you will think, *Obviously, this is the soundtrack of our imminent and deep romantic affair. Thank you for finally finding me, fellow lover of Tom Waits. I have been sending this growling, atonal, screechy birdcall out for YEARS now, hoping you would finally hear it and come to me.*

But what you will actually say is, "Oh, this is the album *Swordfishtrombones* by Tom Waits."

And she will say, "Aha. I wanted to know what it was so that I would never accidentally buy it."

And then she will laugh and leave you alone with your jazzbo carny music for lonely boys.

That will be the first time you realize that some people *do not like Tom Waits.* This is OK. It is not your place in life to convince them otherwise. A job is not a place to curate culture for others or convince them you are as strange and interesting as Elton John's percussionist. You are just there to sell the cheese.

VIDEO STORE CLERK

You cannot work in a video rental store anymore. That is too bad, because it would have been the best job you ever had. It certainly was mine.

The video store I worked in was below street level on Chapel Street in New Haven. I worked there during college, on afternoons and weekends all of one dark, highly air-conditioned summer. The store was called Film Fest, but it was a very quiet fest. We only had two busy periods. The first was in the morning, collecting the returned tapes from the bin and checking them in. The second was in the evening, when people would come to get movies to watch after dinner. Otherwise it would be pretty much me and Patrick or Susan or Sarah or Jacob, sitting around, watching movies.

I don't want to harp on what an education in storytelling and acting that was, because I do not ever, ever want you to confuse me with Quentin Tarantino. However, it *was* that, and also an important reminder that if you can get a job where you are paid to absorb the culture that you love, take that job. Sometimes we would just watch bad movies, because why not? We were young and immortal and had all the time in the world to waste on bad culture, and like bad jobs, bad movies teach you what good things are. We'd watch so many movies that you'd notice themes. For example, in the '80s and '90s, there were many movies starring the actor Bill Pullman in which he is confused, conned, drugged, or betrayed. He gets conned by his wife, Linda Fiorentino, in *The Last Seduction*. He gets conned by his wife again in *Malice*, and also framed for attacking her. He gets framed for murder in *The Serpent and the Rainbow*, then gets sprayed with zombie powder and buried alive. It just goes on and on. You could curate a whole, actual Film Fest featuring only movies in which Bill Pullman gets conned and confused, and the best thing to do would be to invite Bill Pullman to this festival and give him the wrong address. Someday.

Between the busy periods you might see only one customer. But if you're very lucky, that one customer might be an actor, one of the stars of a very, very famous family comedy from the late sixties. But he is not on television anymore. He will be in town because he is acting in a play at the nearby regional theater center. He will come in and you will both act like you don't immediately recognize him from his most and only famous role, the one that has followed him for the rest of his life, all the way into this store. He will ask you where the classic movies are, and you will point them out. He will come back with some seriously classic black-and-white movies and open an account. He will offer his ID, but you don't need to see it. You know who he is.

Then you will break and finally say, *I would love an autograph*, and he will graciously give you one. Then he will take a deep breath and ask you if you also carry adult movies. There will be silence then. It will be you and this famous person alone in the empty, dark, cold video store and universe: he, lonely in a dumpy small American city, touring in a play, just looking for some desperate distraction in his bad hotel room and forced to embarrass himself in front of a college kid to get it; you, that college kid, feeling so bad for your television friend, appreciating this awful position he's in and now knowing that you have to tell him that this whole errand, the whole act he had put on of asking for and renting serious black-and-white movies to cover for his real desire (honestly, this was maybe the best acting he's ever done), was all for nothing. Because you do not carry adult films. You have to go to Best Video in Hamden for that.

I don't know why I'm protecting this guy's privacy. He did

nothing wrong. We're all human, and it's difficult to be human sometimes, especially if you're Greg Brady. But of course this will never happen to you, because there is the internet now. Greg Brady can get any kind of movie he wants now, without talking to anyone, because there are no more video stores.

Easy jobs are great. And as you ease into them, they get even better. They do not challenge you, and you never want to leave. But be careful about getting stuck in the easy jobs. Days turn to years quickly when you are not challenged, frightened, tested. And then maybe someone will invent Netflix.

DISHWASHER

In summers I would go home to Boston and get more jobs. When I was twenty, I worked as a dishwasher at a small restaurant in the Combat Zone.

The Combat Zone was Boston's red-light district. That is a euphemism for "strip club and pornographic movie theater area." I don't need to tell you what porn is (filmed hugging and kissing). You're thirteen and probably have the internet. But I will say that sex and desire and wanting to look at nude people hugging and kissing are natural, powerful instincts that can also be fun when you're not hurting another person. But the ethics and risks of sex work are many and complicated, and, as Cindy Gallop explained in her TED Talk, "Make Love, Not Porn," porn is different from the way most people in the actual world have actual sex. Her talk is four minutes long, and you have my permission to watch it. That is all I will contribute to your sex education. Now show this section to your parents and tell them I say: "You're welcome."

The Combat Zone is gone now, but even then it was fading. Only two clubs and one movie theater, I think, were left. Not much else was happening either. The Downtown Cafe was one of only two operating businesses on an otherwise post-apocalyptically empty block. The other business was an old-fashioned bespoke gentlemen's hat store called Hand the Hatter, its stenciled letters casting shadows on a few dusty hats in its display window. The Hatter never ever seemed to be open, and felt more like a front for a crime operation or maybe a super-secret spy base. But it was not a secret hugging-and-kissing business, and neither was the Downtown.

The Downtown was a small restaurant with maybe twenty seats and an open kitchen in the back. But when I say "open kitchen," please do not think of a sleek, Property Brothers open-concept house in Toronto. It was more like an '80s family dining room with salmon-colored walls, and there was also a dark and banged-up kitchen, and the wall between them had fallen down. The chef and owner was Dan, who looked like a potbellied Rasputin. Dan was gay, and the restaurant was listed in many travel guides for gay men. Essentially it was an openly gay restaurant, and this will surprise you now, but that was probably why, in 1991, it was exiled to the Combat Zone.

Dan did all the cooking and laughing and yelling in front of his battered six-top range. He would flirt with the customers and talk to the feral cats who wandered in the door he kept open to the back garden of vines and weeds. The waiter was a man who was also gay, named Luigi, but everyone called him "Weedge." I write it that way so you know how to pronounce his nickname, but the correct spelling was actually WEGE. I knew this because that's what his tattoo said: W, E, G, E, one letter each beneath the knuckles of his right hand. WEGE had a day job as a jewelry appraiser at a pawn shop around the corner, but he worked at the Downtown for cash tips and fun.

I worked in the back room, pouring the fountain sodas and scraping dishes and loading them into the industrial dishwasher. I learned many things there. I learned the pleasure of solving the jigsaw puzzle of loading the dishwasher efficiently, and I am still the best in the world at that. I learned how to see if a credit card had been canceled by cross-checking it against the bad account numbers listed in the little oblong book the credit card companies sent us every week. I learned how to dress a salad with a squeeze of lemon instead of vinegar, and how to bread and fry a chicken cutlet in butter. I also learned not to eat a customer's discarded chicken cutlet, retrieved from the trash can on a hungry, impishly perverse impulse, because that will make you sick with the flu for two days.

When it got late and dinner service was over, sometimes a few club dancers, friends of Dan's, would stop by after their shifts. Dan would dislodge a four-gallon tub of yellow vanilla ice cream from the packed freezer and make them milk shakes. They would all have a milk shake party in Dan's kitchen, and

Dan would laugh and yowl along with them and the night-yowling cats outside. It was a good time.

Now that I think of it, maybe it wasn't the end of the dancers' shifts. Maybe it was the beginning of their shifts. I never knew. It was not my world. I can't imagine dancing fully or semi-nude onstage directly after pounding a vanilla milk shake. But they were the professionals. I trusted that they knew what they were doing. And even though it wasn't my world, they were all very nice to me.

One night when the dancers weren't around, I sat with Dan and had a Diet Coke as he counted the night's receipts.

"Sometimes, you just have to throw your parents out of the house," he said. Dan was always offering me advice. He was always wondering what this straight boy from Brookline was looking for in a gay kitchen in the Combat Zone. He made no conclusions as far as I remember. The Combat Zone was not a place of judgment.

Tonight, we were talking about my friend Aliza, who had previously waited tables at the Downtown and had gotten me the job. She was having problems with her dad.

"Everyone is scared of their parents kicking *them* out of the house. But sometimes your mom and dad are just wrong. Sometimes, you have to kick them out of the house *first*."

This was something you learn, I guessed, when you grow up gay in Catholic Boston in the 1970s. Maybe it is still true. But Dan's advice was blasphemy to me: I loved my mom and dad!

Once, when I was fifteen, I told my parents no, I did not

think I would accompany them to the Lionel Richie concert on the family date we had all planned. I thought maybe I would go out with my teenage friends instead. This made them very upset, and I continued to live with that guilt.

But Dan's words stuck with me. Later, on my twenty-first birthday, I was back in New Haven. I had driven down the night before to visit a friend. I was supposed to drive back that evening to celebrate my birthday with my parents. But then I decided I didn't want to. *Time to throw them out*, I thought. When I called my mom to tell her that I didn't want to spend my twenty-first birthday with my mom and dad but instead wanted to be in another state and buy alcohol legally with a twenty-one-year-old friend, she got furious and then cried.

I didn't understand at the time. *I'm only throwing you out of the house!* I thought. *Just like my boss/gay fake dad told me to!* But now I get it. Now that I am a parent, I realize this is not what Dan meant. You should definitely go home for your birthday!

But it is true that when you choose a job for yourself, your mom and dad may not like it. It may not be what they pictured for you. They have a lot of time and money invested in you, and they also probably love and care for you. They may not understand at first why you might want to be a gay owner of a gay restaurant, or a gay pawnshop jeweler/waiter. They may not understand that, in fact, you have no choice about these things. But your life is your house, and sometimes you have to kick them out of it.

That said, generally speaking, if you can convince them that you can support yourself and protect yourself, that you are doing the work you love and that you are safe and happy, they will probably be OK with it after a while. Especially if you are not taking money from them. Then you are still living in *their* house.

A little coda to this advice. A couple of times at the end of our shift, Dan asked me to drive WEGE home. WEGE lived in South Boston, which is a traditionally Irish American neighborhood not famed for its tolerance, at least not then. WEGE needed a ride home when it was very late because he was concerned about getting beaten up before he could get inside. But he would never move, he told me. This was where he grew up. This was where he lived with his mother and cared for her. I gave him a ride and watched as he walked to the door. He got home safely.

I realized then you don't *have* to throw your mom and dad out of the house. It's not mandatory. You can, if you want, just live with your mom and dad forever. This is not advice for you, weird thirteen-year-old reader. I'm writing this for my own children.

RECEPTIONIST

The job I got after college was at a literary agency. It fit a number of good-job criteria that I have already established. For one, it was in a beautiful building that I liked walking up to.

Specifically, it was in an old brownstone on Twenty-Sixth Street in Manhattan that had once been a private bank. It was built to house part of the fortune of John Jacob Astor, and it had a walk-in safe with a comically huge and heavy door with a big dial on it. I enjoyed hauling that huge door open and standing in the silent weight of that thick-walled room. It used to safeguard stacks of cash, but now those steel cubbies guarded only unpublished novels, the most worthless paper in the world. It was fun to actually stand in the midst of literal literary irony.

My first job at the agency was to sit at the front desk. I would answer and route telephone calls and sort and distribute faxes. It was a different sort of traffic counting. But it was warm and sheltered (another good job criterion) and I got to sit in a beautiful tiled outer lobby with a gigantic fern that conveyed sophistication. I mentioned there were faxes, because I am old. There was also paper mail. Every day would bring submissions, book proposals, sometimes whole novels printed and boxed and bound and sent blindly by some aspiring author somewhere. Each was a desperate dream. If they weren't addressed to a specific agent, it was my job to read and evaluate them.

It takes a lot to write a novel. You can't just talk about what your job was when you were twenty-two or whatever. You have to make up a whole world from your head, and because first novels are only sold once they are fully written, that requires time and anxiety and the impossible faith that anyone cares. Notice how I have never done it: not even I am that narcissistic. It's an extra cruelty to unpublished novelists that the result of all this labor would be put in my hands, a twenty-two-year-old receptionist, to count like so many turning cars and almost universally reject.

That said, most of these submissions were terrible. I realized from reading them that it takes the same amount of effort to write a good novel as a bad one, and you really don't know which kind you've written until you're done. Writing a novel is a terrible job, but if you absolutely have to do it, here is the only writing advice I ever give: It is not enough to write what you know. You have to know *interesting things*. You have to get out there and learn them. That's where having had a bunch of jobs comes in handy.

I only ever passed along two books to actual agents for consideration. One was a business book called *How to Load Good Trucks*. It was about loading pallets into trucks efficiently, and how that could be a metaphor for executive management techniques. I was only ever confused by business, but I had fond memories of trucks, so I passed it along in honor of Dominic, who liked the movie *Ladyhawke*. The other was a sophisticated thriller set in several countries in Europe. I don't remember much about it except that the protagonist was really into ultra-light aircraft, which are basically motorized kites you sit in. I had always been fascinated by them and remember feeling a genuine sense of tingling happiness at the end. There are a lot of excuses you can make for bad or boring writing. You want books to succeed, so you overlook a lot of dullness and off-notes, plowing through patiently to honor the author's effort.

But you don't have to be patient when you are enjoying something, even if you never thought you would enjoy the genre of International Ultralight Thriller. There's no arguing with a genuine tingle along your forearms and scalp when you reach the end and the protagonist and his girlfriend are double-ultralighting into some foreign sunset. So I passed it along.

But no agent wanted either of these books. If you wrote either (or both!?), I'm sorry it didn't work out.

But when I was not crushing dreams, I enjoyed the job. I was friends with all the other young assistants, and the older agents treated me with kindness. Soon I was promoted to be an assistant and given other responsibilities I was in no way trained for, such as managing the phone system and commenting on legal contracts.

I was not paid much, but I had known what I was getting into. I was compensated in other ways. I got to meet Bruce Campbell. I got to be taken out to lunch by young book editors who also didn't know what they were doing. We would eat food, encouraged by our indulgent bosses, who saw in us not the future of their industry (nonexistent) but their own past. I had health care and free coffee and a sense of belonging.

I took naps on the floor of my boss's office. I am certain she knew this. If she didn't, I'm sorry, Susan. Thank you for your trust in me. You were a great boss. It is a gift to work in an office if you are supported, encouraged, and forgiven. That was why I liked the literary agency and that was why I worked there for seven years. But it was the worst job I ever had.

I was happy, but I was sad. Unlike traffic counting, I knew why I was doing the job, even if I couldn't confess it to myself. I worked there because I wanted to be a writer, but I was afraid to join that pile of dreams that slushed onto my desk every day. So I comforted myself by being *around* writers, and to some degree helping them, but mostly taking parasitic pleasure in their company, and also a portion of their income. Ultimately it was a sales job, involving a friendly style of conflict called "negotiation" that only ever terrified me. The longer I worked there, the more scared I was that I would work there forever.

But quitting was still scarier. The future is uncertain. You are afraid you will let people down, or that they'll be angry at you for leaving. But most people don't think about you that much, except for your moms or dads or guardians. If you read my last book you may know that it took the untimely death of my mother to shake me out of the delusion that my job was more important than my life. If my children were ever trapped in the same unhappiness and I knew my death would help them escape it, I would welcome that fate.

But I will not die for you, weird thirteen-year-old. I don't like you *that* much. I will only say that the worst jobs are not the hardest jobs. The worst job is the job you know is wrong for you, but you stay in it anyway.

Since the literary agency I have only ever worked for myself as a writer and performer or whatever I am. You know about all these jobs. I've done well in some and worse in others. I've loaded some good trucks and some bad ones. But I know I am doing all that I am capable of doing, all that I can't *not* do, and I am paid for it. It is the best job I have ever had.

YOUNG ADULT AUTHOR

One thing I learned from my time at the literary agency is that books for children and young adults tend to be shorter than novels. They don't always work, but the risk-to-reward ratio is much more reasonable. And when kids' books do succeed, man, that's where the money is. But I never had a topic for a young adult book until now, and I just wrote it. I like to think we did it together (even though I get all the money)! Good job.

Chapter Ten

AWARDS SEASON

The writer Neil Gaiman tells a story about impostor syndrome, and there's really no better story about that subject, so I'm going to steal it. Sorry, Neil.

Neil had been invited to a secret meeting of interesting people, writers, scientists, poets laureate, adventurers, etc. None of them knew why they had been invited. The man who organized it simply said he wanted to meet them all, which only made it more suspicious and strange-feeling. I won't tell you where it was except to say it might as well have been on a crater on the dark side of the moon, that is how confused and out of place everyone felt there. (I was not invited.)

At one point, Neil was standing in the back of a room next to an older gentleman.

"I just look at all these people, and I think, what the heck am I doing here? They've made amazing things," the older gentleman said. "I just went where I was sent."

That is when Neil Gaiman pointed out that the older

gentleman was Neil Armstrong, and that surely must count for something.

And that is when Neil Armstrong said, "Oh, right! NO WONDER THIS CRATER ON THE DARK SIDE OF THE MOON LOOKS SO FAMILIAR! Look, there are the space cuff links I dropped the last time I was here... *many moons ago!* Get it? Many *moons* ago? Why aren't you laughing, you gothy weirdo? That's solid wordplay!"

Obviously Neil Armstrong did not actually say that last part. I made that up, and frankly it makes the story better. Even a Neil Gaiman story needs some punch up, now and again.

But the rest of the story is all true, and when Neil tells it (and boy, does he tell it—so often that it's basically in the public domain), he uses it to reassure people that everyone, even the most accomplished people in their respective fields (writing stories and/or walking on the moon and/or making moon puns), feel like impostors. This is very comforting to hear, and mostly it is true. But not always.

I learned this when the TV show was renewed for a second season, and I was invited back to be on it again. I flew back to LA to see my pretend friends again. But now we were *actual* friends, or as much as we could be. Movie- and TV-set friendships are like summer camp friendships: You are thrown together in some other world and bond intensely over long days and confessional nights until the night of the final party. And then you hug and say you will stay in touch, and you part, never to see, talk to, or think about each other again. Unless you come back.

Our final scene of the first season had in fact been a party: a pretend barbecue in my Leading Best Friend and his Leading Best Wife's backyard. My Leading Best Friend cooked the same hamburgers over and over as we said our final lines. And when all the dialogue was done, we were supposed to take these burned burger lumps and smile and eat them and then break out into a planned spontaneous dance party.

By the way, if you ever have to film a backyard barbecue, I would advise you not to improvise and pick up a huge plastic bowl of cheese balls at the beginning of the scene and shove a handful in your mouth. It doesn't matter how much you love cheese balls (which in my case was *all* the much) and how fondly you remember them from your teenage days digging trenches. Because you are not a teenager anymore, and once you eat them in the wide shot of the scene, you are committed to eating them for take after take after take as they cover every angle. You have to eat a new handful of cheese balls over and over again, and then it is time for you to dance in the hot sun. And by then, at the end of summer camp, you love your pretend friends and the dancing and laughing is real. But so are the cheese balls in your stomach. The cheese balls are very, very real.

We started the second season with a party as well, but we were not in a backyard anymore. We were in a mansion. A wealthy Other Best Friend (I guess I was on to the Secretary of State of Best Friendship in the order of succession now) was throwing Leading Best Wife a fortieth-birthday party. It was an actual, beautiful large home, and the production took it over, replacing all the family photographs with fake family photographs. The party stretched from the marble foyer to the huge open kitchen, through the french doors and out to the patio and pool. Dozens of background actors milled back and forth from foyer to pool as we shot the scene. My job was to stand by the kitchen counter and drink grape juice instead of wine and chat with Leading Best Wife.

I realize that "Leading Best Wife" is wrong and demeaning, since the character is a whole human being in her own right, and also because she was played by Judy Greer, who is a wonderful actor and human whom I love. Any time you say the name "Judy Greer" in Hollywood, everyone around you will say, "I *love* Judy Greer." I mean: everyone, every time. You can even say "Judy Greer" in an empty room and someone will appear to say, "Judy Greer is the best!" It's a little unnerving. It's as if everyone in entertainment has been given some *Manchurian Candidate*–style posthypnotic instruction to say this. But it happens to be true. Now it was great to see her again in the mansion by the kitchen counter, and since we were just in background in this moment, we caught up on our lives and pets and children, like actual human beings at an actual party.

The woman who had directed me at the haunted house was back, and it was great to see her as well. I honestly was grateful for her efforts to make me smaller and more natural, and I wanted to show her that I was better at acting now. But I really wasn't. I kept looking into the camera. This is a bad thing to do when your primary job is to pretend that cameras do not exist.

But I had come up through *The Daily Show*, where all we did was stare into the camera, and I had gotten very good at it. Time after time, I would turn around to face the main action of the scene, and my eyes would instantly find that camera and bore into it.

"Cut," the Director would say. She would take me aside. "You're looking in the camera, John."

"I know," I would say. "I'm sorry."

And then I'd do it again. On each new shot, even when the camera changed positions when I wasn't looking, I would find it somehow. This is bad enough in a small scene between two or three people. But it is especially bad when you are shooting a big party scene with dozens of background actors who need to stop their fake milling and weird silent party chatter and be sent back to their starting positions every time your eyes find the accusing, blank lens. It's also not good when your director has to be at the airport first thing in the morning and now first thing in the morning is in two hours.

Eventually we reached the point when everyone was supposed to run out of the kitchen in shocked surprise as Judy Greer and Leading Best Friend jumped into the pool, fully clothed, on a mutual dare. OK, I realize now that Leading Best Friend is going to be mad that I didn't reveal *his* name, so I'll tell you: his name is Nat Faxon, and he is also the best. So is Brett Gelman. Are you happy now, you guys?

In any case, Judy and Nat were pretending to jump into the pool, and the Director was shooting this scene from far away, hidden somewhere in the patio bushes. They did not show me where the camera was. I stood in my spot in the kitchen when I heard "action," and then I ran out onto the patio with a surprised look on my face (acting). I wasn't looking anywhere in particular.

"Cut," the Director called from somewhere in the night. "You're looking in the camera!" she said.

"How?!" I said in angry frustration with myself. "I don't even know where it is!" I couldn't see it even now. I guess I was just that good.

Finally, before dawn, Judy and Nat got into the pool. We were approaching the martini—the last shot of the night. Once your lead goes into the water, there's not much you can shoot after that. The Director filmed their words and faces as they bobbed in the pool, and then she turned the camera around to the other side of the pool to shoot me and my reaction to this wacky turn of events. The camera was right there, across the pool, beckoning my stupid eyes.

"Don't look in the camera, John," said Nat from the pool. The scene was shot without sound, and his face was not on camera, so he could say whatever he wanted. He smiled and said, over and over, "Don't do it. Don't you do it, John. Don't look in the camera. Hey, John. Don't."

I've never felt smaller. But I didn't mind. The sun was coming up, and he was doing me a favor. If he hadn't been there to distract me, I totally would have looked in that camera. I would have ruined the shot for everyone there. I would have climbed into that lens and died. But I didn't. The Director made her flight, my best friends dried off. We got the martini shot, but I didn't have a martini because it was dawn.

We all feel like impostors sometimes. Because we are. We don't get anywhere without a little overreach, without faking it a little. This is especially true if your job is to literally pretend to be another person. But even if it's not, it's good to be in over your head sometimes, as life is enriched by terror and surviving it.

However, some of us *are* impostors, or at least are so good at faking competence that we stray over the border into legitimate incompetence. There is a lot of hand-wringing about call-out culture these days, especially among white guys whose mediocrity has traditionally been only rewarded, and whose perspective was for a long time presumed to be universal truth, rather than the one narrow sliver of experience left visible to them through all their many blind spots. But now I know it's a gift to be called out. It's a gift when someone takes you aside and tells you that you are not a good actor, for example; that you are an impostor even in the art of faking it. It's a gift because they don't *have* to tell you this; they may even be punished for it. And while it is painful to hear, it gives you the chance to do better. It reminds you that when you actually and genuinely do a good job and you know it, no one can lie to you.

Some months later, at the premiere party for the show's second season, I saw the Director and thanked her. I thanked her for pushing me, and for caring about the work enough to do so. I told her it wasn't always easy to hear her criticism, and I am sure it was not fun to have to offer it. But I do think it helped. Over the course of the season I did some pretty good work singing Korean karaoke, and later I got to be mean to a child, and then I had a monologue where my character had to reflect upon his own childhood. "Mommy was right," I said. "I don't deserve love." I got pretty small, and I think I did OK.

Now that I write this, I don't remember if the Director actually agreed with my self-assessment. But I'm still grateful to her.

Around this time I went back to spend a few nights at the Hotel again. I don't remember why I didn't stay with Paul and Janie. Maybe they had a guest already. Or maybe I just couldn't stay away.

It was awards season in Los Angeles. In fact, the Golden Globes were taking place on the afternoon I arrived, and that night there was a glamorous private party in the Hotel's garden. I knew it happened because I heard the party through my window. I was not invited.

I had found out about the party when I checked in that afternoon. My room wasn't ready, so I sat in the lobby. While I was waiting, I was delivered a coffee I hadn't ordered. I pointed this out to the server, who apologized. He said he was sorry, realized his mistake, and brought it over to Gary Oldman. This made me very happy. It felt like it was going to be a good visit.

Then Paul Rudd came in and saw me. He asked me if I was going to the party, and I said, "I don't know what you're talking about."

And Paul Rudd said, "Oh. Well. Uh."

I didn't mind. Paul Rudd was adorable about it, just as he is adorable about all things, always. And frankly, I wasn't surprised I hadn't been invited, because frankly, I didn't matter. I was the vice-vice-vice best friend on a smaller cable comedy. It had been a long time since my version of celebrity had amounted to much in the Hollywood fame ledger. But one of the things I always liked about the Hotel was that it kept a second, *secret* ledger: a private, off-the-books accounting of novelists and odd-balls and lively washed-ups and weirds that they just *liked* for some reason, and for a while, you could find my name there.

Because I was on this secret list, the Hotel would always find a room for me, even on the night of the Golden Globes. Usually when I checked in, there was a note of hello from Phil, the general manager, and a bottle of the gin I like, which I would then take down to donate to the bar. Sometimes I would notice, on the second or third day, that one of my own books had been placed on the bookshelf. And from time to time over the years when I checked in, Phil would randomly bump me upstairs to a room with a balcony where I could see a double rainbow that I presume he also arranged somehow. I liked Phil. I had come to appreciate his magic act of making everyone feel like they are the only person on earth. I wonder if the fact that, unlike many of his guests, I didn't actually *believe* I was the only human on earth was part of why he liked me back. I hope so.

"Well," said Paul Rudd, "you should just come down anyway. You'll know people. No one will stop you."

"Oh no," I said. "It's fine." And it was. Because even though I had not been invited, I knew I would be going anyway. Because along with the gin and note of welcome, whenever the Hotel had a private party, they would usually leave a note in their guests' rooms saying, effectively: *You can come to the party anyway, because we love you.*

But once my room was ready and I checked in, there was no note saying that I could go to the party anyway. I looked and looked and looked. I called Phil. He explained that they had asked the host of the party if she would mind if a bunch of strangers she didn't know, people that the Hotel likes but who have otherwise been rejected by culture, could just go ahead and crash the party she was paying for. Strangely, the host said no, thank you. It was as if the host wanted to actually choose her own company! Phil seemed as confused about it as I was, or at least knew to act that way.

The party was going to take over both the lobby and the patio—all the public space in the Hotel. "But you know," he said, "you should just go down anyway. No one will stop you."

"Oh no," I said. "It's fine." But now it was *not* fine. At all. Being on television may have made me into a monster in some ways, but if I was a monster, I was a vampire: I will come and leech your life force and delicious fame blood to restore my power and revive the shambling, shrunken Nosferatu of my relevance. *But you have to invite me in first.* I'm not some hairy fame werewolf who's going to burst in and maraud the place just because nobody stopped me.

I *had* to be invited, especially and painfully since I had worked with the host once or twice. Even if I could hide my sad fame-hunger from myself (I'm pretty good at hiding from myself), *she* would see it the moment I walked in. And the idea of not going to the party at all was too terrible to think about. I did not want to believe the party, the ongoing, years-long party at this hotel and beyond to which I had never expected to be invited but could now be over. Or worse: *going on without me.*

I sent emails to various agents and in-betweens I knew, asking them if they could get me on the list. I sent texts to people I knew who might be going, hoping they would make me their plus one. I waited for hours. Nothing came back.

I already had plans to have dinner with a friend. It was a nice dinner, but I stretched it out as long as I could. I had a plan in the back of my mind that if I got back to the Hotel *just* late enough, I would run into someone I knew as they were going into the party. They would say to me, "Of course you are invited, are you crazy? *I'm* inviting you," and then they would sweep me in with them and I would be welcome again.

But the party was still hours away by the time I got back. The lobby was empty except for a group of serving people being briefed by their supervisor on the various passed appetizers. I could have gone into the lobby then and hidden behind a plant, to emerge later when the party began. No one would have stopped me. But I went upstairs to my room.

Maybe someone would call me before long and let me know, at the last minute, that I *was* invited. I decided to pass the time watching screeners. During awards season, movie studios send out countless DVDs of movies they hope will win awards. I got these screeners because I was a member of the Screen Actors Guild and could vote in their awards ceremony. I don't recall all the movies that were sent to me that year, because there were so many, and of course I had never heard of them before because the studios had made them all in secret.

This was a few years ago, before a science fiction movie about a sexy fishman won best picture and it was still presumed that only super-serious dramas and historical movies could win awards, so Hollywood had a secret program to make them. They made movies about creepy wrestling coaches and problematic jazz instructors designed to show the range of interesting actors and the verve of young directors. This would make the actors and directors feel better about later making big movies about superheroes and Minions and teenagers killing each other in mazes, which actually could be shown to humans. These secret good movies, however, were only meant to win awards, so it was not necessary for normal humans to see them. And at this time, mostly they didn't. The studios made the secret movies and sometimes put them in a movie theater for a day or two. But mostly they just mailed them to Academy voters and members of various acting and writing trade unions to watch. Back then it was so important to Hollywood that the secret movies *stay* secret that the screeners would all come with a warning: THIS IS FOR YOU ONLY. DO NOT SHARE OR SHOW THIS TO ANYONE ELSE. Literally one screener told me that when I was done watching, I should break it in half, lest the secret good movie accidentally get into the wrong hands.

I watched one of these secret movies as the night deepened. Soon I heard the party starting below. I once again had the room I liked with the window above the patio. But now the sexy parent dinner party that used to soothe me only caused me pain. I checked my phone. No one had called or texted or emailed or slipped a last-minute invite under my door. They could not stop me from going down. I would have to stop myself.

I closed the window and put on another movie. And after a long, *long* time, as the party got wild and the laughter of all my famous friends enjoying one another battered at the window like a growing storm, I fell asleep. (I also took some prescription medicine.)

When I woke up the next morning, I felt purified, like I had taken the first step to kicking a dangerous drug. I showered and dressed and went down to the lobby, where I was once again welcome. I ordered coffee and I felt great.

But then three men and their wives sat down on the clutch of sofas next to me. They were all in their midfifties, I would say, wide and genial and good-mannered, so I was not surprised to overhear that they were from Missouri. As they spoke, I gathered that the three men were doctors who had all come to Los Angeles for a medical conference.

They were all staying at the Hotel, which they thought was very lovely, but a little pricey, didn't you think so? Yes, they all agreed. I learned from their conversation that they didn't need to be in the secret book of favored guests to get not one but three rooms at the Hotel on the night of the Golden Globes. One of them just made the reservations online a couple of days ago. Wasn't that very lucky? They all agreed it was.

"Say, Don," said one of the men to one of the others. "Did you know it was the Golden Globes last night?"

"I didn't know that, Dick," said Don. "But that makes sense."

"Yes it does, Don," said Dick, "because Joan and I heard a big party last night, out in the garden."

"Oh, I know all about it," said Don. "You know, Carl and I left the conference later than you did, and when we got back, the party was in full swing."

"Did you and Carl go in to the party, Don?" said Dick.

"Yes, we did," said Don. "We got up here to the lobby and we walked right in."

"Nobody stopped us," Carl agreed.

Don said, "That's right. We just walked in and everyone was nice and we had some champagne off a tray."

"So how was the party?" asked Dick.

"Well, Dick, it was just great. There were a lot of actors here. I spent the longest time talking to Bill Murray. Boy, Bill Murray was just a good, good guy. Did you talk to him, Carl?"

"Just a little, Don," said Carl. "But then I saw Jessica Lange."

"Oh, from *King Kong* and *American Horror Story: Menopause*?" asked Dick.

"That's right, Dick," said Carl. "Boy, is she funny! She really had me laughing! We talked and talked, and then she told me my mustache was tight, and then she kissed me."

"How about that!" said Don. "Well, I am sorry I missed that, Carl. But guess what. It looks like I am going to be in a Wes Anderson movie."

"Really!" said Carl. "Now, just how did that come about, Don?"

"Well," said Don, "I was just talking to this nice young man wearing a corduroy blazer and shorts with tube socks, and he said his name was Wes. And then he said that he thought I might be good for his new movie about a massive indoor water park in Germany that is housed in a former zeppelin factory. He said he was looking for a middle-aged guy with facial hair, someone who could pass for Gary Oldman's fatter, more American cousin."

"Oh," said Carl, "like a John Hodgman type."

"I don't know who that person is, Carl," said Don. "But I guess he wasn't around, because Wes Anderson said I fit the bill, and now I have to join SAG."

"Good for you, Don," said Dick.

"Yeah, good for you," said Carl.

"I am sure glad I went to that party," said Don.

I swear to you that this conversation is only slightly exaggerated. The broad outlines are absolutely true. As I heard them talk about the party, I was glad for them. They really did seem to have had a good time. I was also glad they were doctors, because I felt about ready to slit my wrists with the shards of that abusive-jazz-drums-movie DVD I had broken in half the night before.

That wasn't the very last time I went to the Hotel, but it pretty much was. Phil has left and I don't think I'm in their special book of favored regulars and totally random midwestern doctors anymore. That's OK. It's good to know when you're no longer on the list. There is only sadness in pretending you still are. I didn't want to be an impostor anymore.

Chapter Eleven

BELOVED ONE

Sometime later, it was June. Disneyland was in the distant past, and my family had gone home. It was near the end of the second season of the TV show, and I was finally going home, too.

I took a cab to LAX. I had taken this ride to the Beloved Airlines door many times: flopping out of the car at the priority passenger door at Terminal 5 and rolling through TSA all Platinum-ed out was like putting on an old pair of gifting-lounge jeans to me. But when I got out of the car this time, I saw a *new* door. I had never noticed it before, and I stood in the unloading zone staring at it: a new magic door barred by frosted sliding glass, with the words "BELOVED ONE" above it.

I knew that Beloved Airlines had begun rebranding its first class service as Beloved One. I knew I was flying first class. I knew that if I went to that door and was turned away, I would feel bad. I would walk back into traffic and wait until something hit me. But I had to find out. It called to me.

I walked to the door, and a man appeared. I mean it. Appeared. He was holding a tablet.

"May I go through this door?" I asked. "Am I in Beloved One?"

He asked me my name, and I told him. He checked the tablet. My name was on it.

"Welcome, Mr. Hodgman," said the tablet bearer.

The frosted doors slid open, and I entered a white room with a white marble floor. There was nothing in it except a silver airplane wing that had been made into a desk. Standing behind the desk were a man and a woman. The man was stocky and smiled. The woman was tall and kind. She said, "Hello. We are here to help you."

All of this is true.

The woman asked me for my boarding pass. "It's on my phone," I said.

"I'll take it," she said. "And your ID." I surrendered them.

The smiling man came around the desk that was a wing. "Are you checking this bag?"

"Yes," I said.

He nodded. He attached a luggage tag to it.

"Thank you," I said. "Where is the conveyor belt? I'll put it on."

"There is no conveyor belt," he said. "Come with me."

"What about my phone and my ID?" I asked.

"You do not need those things anymore," he said. "Don't worry about anything. Come with me."

I did. He led me around the corner to a lounge. "I know this place," I said. "It's a Sky Lounge."

It was. It was an impossible, double-secret Sky Lounge on the departures level. There were sleek, Windexable armchairs. Side tables with discreet USB outlets. A long table with tea sandwiches and upscale potato chips and urns of cucumber water. The room was empty.

The smiling man told me to wait here, and I waited. I had some cucumber water. I ate a sandwich. I didn't see another human. I wondered, *Wait. Maybe I'm not* IN *Beloved One. Maybe I am* THE *Beloved One.*

The tall, warm woman clicked back on her heels. She handed me a paper boarding pass, my phone, and my ID. She gestured to a silver elevator I had not noticed. "When you are ready, you can go up. Until then, just relax."

"Ha ha," I said. "I never relax! Certainly not before I go through security."

She said, "Oh, don't worry. We have our own private security line."

"Oh," I said. "I would like to see that."

"Well," she said, "are you ready to go up?"

I finished my cucumber water. "Yes," I said.

She walked me over to the elevator and pressed the single button. "This is our private elevator," she said. "This will take you up."

"By myself?" I asked.

"I will go with you," she said. "As far as I can."

The door opened, and we got in, and silently, we went up.

The elevator opened on a quiet, empty, white hallway, again with marble floors.

"This way," she said. I followed her. There was no noise, other than the *click, click, click* of her heels on the floor and the *thrum* of my rollerboard's wheels. Once again, we were alone. I wanted to turn to her and confirm what was now obvious, which was that I was dead.

I am dead, right? I wanted to say. *Obviously when I got out of the cab in the loading zone I was immediately hit by another car. And then my spectral form stood up and saw a magic portal in the wall that no one else could see, and then I walked through it, and now I am dead?*

This was a reasonable fear. Airports are terrifying enough, even when you are not flying Beloved One. When you go to an airport, you know that you are *probably* not going to die. But all the same, you are deploying your belief in statistics and personal experience against a deeper, equally unmovable force: that you are about to do something that is impossible. You are going to get into a giant, heavy steel tube full of people and their farts, and that tube is going to levitate until it is thousands of feet above the earth, to a point where, should the tube fail, the pressure difference would suck you out of the tube into temperatures that would instantly kill you. You are going to be inside of the tube, and people on the ground will look up and see your tube, a thin silver toothpick full of souls, spreading its contrails, and they will not think, *It's John Hodgman!* You will be microscopic, beyond reach, nothing. Which is somehow more suffocating and terrifying to think of, for me, than dying in a fiery crash.

Still, you have to get somewhere. You have to get to Columbus, Ohio, to attend a ceremony for a prize you are going to lose. (Just as an example.) And so airports are designed to distract you from your existential dread, specifically by making you angry. They treat you like animals, running you through endless SensaBand mazes and weird psychological tests. Gate agents invite "passengers needing a little extra help" to board first, knowing that they are prohibited from being more specific, knowing that they cannot challenge anyone claiming disability. And then the gate agents watch as the crowd sizes one another up, wondering which among them will have the craven courage to fake a limp, or pretend their carry-on is an oxygen tank, or present their asthmatic pug as a service animal. Which one will be first to abandon civilization so they can get on the fart tube early so that they can arrive in Columbus at the exact same time as everyone else?

And of course they denude and degrade you. They make you take your shoes off even though we all know it is dumb, and they touch your body at will, if only to remind you that we do not live in a society of laws, but a society of power . . . only to remind you that you are willing to trade your human dignity to get to Columbus on a November afternoon to lose a prize and spend a bone-cold night missing your family, and then to surrender your dignity once more, just to fly home, on the verge of tears the entire time. (A hypothetical.)

Most important, airports put you in close proximity to *other* angry humans, so you can focus on *their* despicable habits and get furious with them. Because as pointless and humiliating as taking your shoes off is, at least *I* am very good at it, unlike *you*, adorable grandmom or teenager in front of me. Your technique is awful. Don't wait until your bag has gone through and then act surprised when told you have to take off your shoes. We have been doing this for almost twenty years. Are you truly telling me that you have not flown in twenty years? Now, wait. Why are you walking back from the body scanner? You didn't take your phone out of your pocket? How do you even know how to use a phone without knowing this? WHY ARE YOUR POCKETS FULL OF OLD FOIL GUM WRAPPERS AND SPARE SIG-NET RINGS? WHY ARE YOU BRINGING NINE DOLLARS IN CHANGE INTO THE AIRPORT? ARE YOU REALLY WEARING AN EXOSKELETON RIGHT NOW? LIKE FROM THE MOVIE *ALIENS*? THIS IS NO TIME FOR COSPLAY!

This is all on purpose. Because while you are mind-yelling at everyone around you, you do not think about anything else. But when they take away all signifiers of "airport-ness"—when they take away the lines and the conveyor belts, when they take away the other people and your hatred of them—and you just have a smiling person saying to you, *Give me your possessions. You don't need them anymore. I will take care of you. I will take you up*, it is hard not to think you are dead. When you *click*,

click, click farther down a bone white hall to a private security screening area that is completely, impossibly empty, it is difficult not to feel that you have been pre-cleared to enter oblivion.

But then the tall woman said to me, "I'm sorry. I forgot that our private screening area is not open today. May I take you in to regular security?"

She gestured to a door. On the other side, I heard voices— complaining, crying, protesting, indignant, stupid, hateful other people. I was so relieved. I felt like George Bailey finding Zuzu's petals in his pocket. I was alive. "Yes, please," I said.

She took me through the door to the regular line. "I can walk you to the front of this line," she said. "Would you be comfortable with that?"

"Of course," I said. "It will be just like when I go to Disneyland." And so she walked me past everyone in line and waved her pass at the TSA agent.

"This is as far as I can take you," she said.

I understood. I put my bag through the X-ray and took off my shoes (I was not yet TSA PreCheck). I did it really well, and I *also* took off my belt because I know how this stuff gets *done*. I know how to reveal my body to a still-experimental booth that bombards you with radiation and takes a picture of your nudity that never goes away no matter what they say. And while I was there, being beautifully scanned, I wondered what would happen when I got through this final portal. Was I really going to just be vomited out into the regular terminal? Or would I be ushered to some new weird luxury, walked into a coffinlike lay-flat seat and sung to by a choir as I was fed the finest tranquilizers and transferred directly onto the plane, like an adult unaccompanied minor in a giant stroller who needs a *little* extra help.

The answer is no. When you are no longer the Beloved One, you are just vomited into the regular terminal. And you will feel like someone who has just had a near-death experience. You want to scream through the terminal, "Heaven is real! I have seen it." But you refrain, because you do not want to be thrown in Airport Jail. Unless, wait: is there a Platinum Jail?

PS: Do not seek the Beloved One portal. it doesn't exist anymore. Soon after this experience, Beloved moved terminals and abandoned the whole expensive Beloved One complex. And soon after this, my TV show was canceled.

Chapter Twelve

JONATHAN AND DREW AND LINUS AND CHOMPERS

One time I was invited to a party in Adam Savage's secret workshop. Adam Savage used to be a MythBuster on the show *MythBusters*. But his passion has always been prop replication. This means he would take his mythbusting money and funnel it into, say, building a perfect replica of the Maltese Falcon from *The Maltese Falcon*, using the actual materials they would have used in 1941 to make actual Maltese falcons. I don't know what those materials are. Vintage falcon malt, I guess. Ask him.

Adam has also made perfect replicas of Rasputin's gauntlet from *Hellboy* and Tom Skerritt's space suit from *Alien*. He has made Deckard's blaster from *Blade Runner* not once, but three times for himself and six times for others. He makes these things and hides them behind a blank door on a side street in San Francisco, along with Jason Bourne's identity kit from *The Bourne Identity* and Major Kong's survival kit from *Dr. Strangelove* and space helmets of every kind. Han Solo in carbonite hangs on the wall not far from a mournful, full-size Chewbacca. Over by a vintage *Centipede* cabinet stands Admiral Ackbar, but now Admiral Ackbar is dressed in a British naval uniform from the Napoleonic Wars—a perfect replica of Russell Crowe's uniform from *Master and Commander*. Attack ships on fire off the shoulder of Orion. C-beams glittering in the dark near the Tannhäuser Gate. I have seen things you people wouldn't believe.

He calls his workshop his "cave." Every January in San Francisco there is a great comedy festival called SF Sketchfest, and Adam opens the unmarked door and invites the comedians inside. It is a very popular party. R2D2 passes out drinks like it's Jabba's sail barge and Adam sits and quietly enjoys himself as all these nerd-dude heads explode around him.

I was having a good time at one of these parties, just chilling in a perfect replica of Captain Kirk's chair, sipping on a whiskey and pushing all the buttons and making all the *beep boop* sounds. And then I noticed there were not one but two corgis at this party. Not replicas, but actual corgis being held by their owners in the middle of the room. Corgis, of course, are adorable full-size dogs with deformed, miniature legs. Part of the reason they are so adorable is that they always seem to be cheerful and smiling even though someone chopped their legs off, generations ago, through selective breeding.

I didn't recognize the owners of the corgis. They weren't comedians. It seemed pretty gross to bring dogs to a nerd party just to get attention, and I didn't like that these corgi owners were getting more attention than me. So I asked my friend Kevin: Who invited *them*?

"Oh, *they* weren't invited," he said. "The corgis were." Kevin explained that they were famous corgis on Instagram. One of Kevin's colleagues was a big fan, so he contacted the owners and invited them to this party. I learned that one of the Corgis is named Linus, and the other is named Chompers, and I'm going to go ahead and say the first and last name of the man who invited dogs to a party because I want him to be known: Conor Lastowka.

Later I would do some research on these dogs. Not surprisingly, Chompers is more famous than Linus, because Chompers is an incredible name for an Instagram corgi. Chompers has 132,000 followers on Instagram as of this writing, whereas Linus has only around 15,000. On his Instagram account, Chompers does co-branded poses with vacuum cleaners and boutique pet food companies. But Linus has the more impressive pedigree: His sire is Ch. Misty Ridge Rumblestiltskin, and his dam is Ch. Brnayr Fancy Pants.

Still, I was not impressed. To clarify, I was invited to the party because I had just performed in the comedy festival. I had stood onstage, on only *two* feet, and spoken words using the power of human speech. Plus, I am able to sweat through my skin, not just through panting. And *these* guys, sorry, these *DOGS*, Linus and Chompers, were invited to the same Adam Savage party, simply because they are DOGS ON THE INTERNET. I don't think even they knew what planet Admiral

Ackbar is *from*. (The answer is Mon Calamari, for all the dumb dogs who are reading this.)

That was when I realized I don't know what entertainment is anymore.

A few months earlier I had gone to the Emmys with *The Daily Show*. It was the last year the show would be nominated with Jon Stewart as host.

It was fun. There were no dogs there. I got myself invited to the HBO after-party and saw George R. R. Martin. It's always enjoyable to party with George R. R. Martin because a GRRM party is a sit-down party, and that's where I am at now.

But the Emmy telecast itself was strange. I had been invited to go with *The Daily Show* to the Emmys for several years, starting in 2008. The hosts that year were Tom Bergeron, Heidi Klum, Howie Mandel, Jeff Probst, and Ryan Seacrest. All of them, onstage, talking over one another. It was the first year the Television Academy offered an award for hosting a reality show, and all five hosts were nominated. Reality television had been dominating traditional scripted television in the ratings for a decade. The success of reality was humiliating, and scripted television had been trying to pretend it wasn't happening. But now the Academy wanted to show they were taking reality television seriously, and they did it by treating each of its biggest stars as one-fifth of a human being.

You have to understand that this was before you were born. This was back when there were only about one hundred television shows and all of them were on traditional television.

There were no pads or apps or streams yet. And when a show won an award, the whole house erupted in applause, because even if it wasn't the show the audience wanted to win, at least they had heard the name of that show at least once in their life.

But this year, my last year, it was clear how much had changed. Now there were roughly one million television shows and most of them were on phones and Facebooks and tablets and Twitters. It is overwhelming. Around this time a producer I knew said, "If I told you that Patrick Stewart, one of the biggest TV stars of all time, was currently starring in a brand-new TV show that is airing on cable right now, would you even be able to name it?"

In fact I *could* name it—*Blunt Talk*—but mostly because I had been in two episodes of it. This producer didn't know this. He hadn't gotten around to seeing it yet. Also, he was my manager at the time.

Before the Emmys this year I had joined the Television Academy. It didn't cost much and it made me feel important. I was surprised to learn that television networks send out screeners to voters as well. Even though most of the two thousand television networks are streaming networks, and all of the 25,000,000,000 nominated shows are available to be called up instantly on any version of any screen, the networks still send their shows out to Academy voters on DVDs.

They print them, package them in five- and ten-packs, entombed in thick folios and heavy cardboard boxes, and ship them out in trucks and airplanes, all across the country and finally to you. Brick after brick of whole seasons of television stack up on your counter, a monument to burnt fuel and spent plastic, a haunting cairn of scripted and unscripted television reminding you that there is more TV than you will ever be able to watch before you die. (And in my case, specifically, it reminds me that even though there are *so many* shows now, none of them want to hire me. That's when I pull the TV cairn down on top of me and hope it crushes me.)

There is no television anymore, but also there is *only* television. And now at the Emmys, there were no more huge applause moments. Just isolated pockets of clapping, like small fireworks cracking over distant hills, far on the other side of the valley, briefly illuminating neighboring towns you were never going to visit.

Here is a nomination for Coach Friday Night Lights for his work on a streaming show that is about a family sitting on a Florida dock with their feet in the water, I guess? the announcer might say, and then: clap, clap over there in the mezzanine.

Here is a nomination for the star of the prison show we called a comedy last year, but this year is a drama because categories are meaningless now and we don't know what TV is anymore! (But at least we can all agree to never mention again how she starred in the first Atlas Shrugged *movie.)*

Clap, clap somewhere behind me. Clap, clap.

Here is a win for Tilda Swinton's secret talk show filmed in the International Space Station and shown exclusively on the seat backs of Japanese bullet trains! (That's not a thing, but it will be.)

Clap. Clap.

It was like listening to the culture fragment in real time.

There were only three moments I recall when the house really exploded with applause. One was when Jon Hamm finally won the Lead Actor Emmy for *Mad Men* after eight nominations. He deserved the standing ovation. He had done a good acting job, tricking all of culture into rooting for a human monster. And also: Jon Hamm.

The second moment wasn't even an award. It was when Taraji P. Henson was introduced as a presenter. This was at the very beginning of *Empire*, and the bomb cyclone of cheers in the room reminded us that, at least for now, there was still a thing called broadcast television, and it reached a *lot* of people. It reminded us that television is not just white people poking at their phones, streaming the reboot of *The Adventures of Brisco County, Jr.* on the Airbnb app. (Again, not a thing. But it will be.) And also: Taraji P. Henson.

And the third was Jon Stewart. Jon had already handed the show over to Trevor Noah at this point, but *The Daily Show with Jon Stewart* was still eligible for the work of the previous year. This was the last time he would be in this room for this job, and it was not a surprise that he won.

The way it works at the Emmys is this: If the show won for writing, the writers would go onstage to receive the award. If the show won its category overall, it was the producers' turn to go up. The cast would typically never go onstage, and I'm talking the regular, full-time correspondents, not just the once-a-monthers like me. This never bothered me. I hate getting up and walking places in general, and it was happier for me to sit back in the empty row of chairs and applaud my friends. I enjoyed the cool of the auditorium and the luxury strangeness of being flown out to LA to not even stand up.

But tonight we had been warned that if *The Daily Show* won, Jon wanted us all onstage. When LL Cool J announced the winner (us), the applause was huge. It shuddered through me, vibrating the hairs on my neck. It was the final round of Emmy applause for Jon's sixteen years hosting the show. It was unquestionably his moment, and we were shy now about joining him onstage. We hesitated. But he looked at us like we were dummies, and he waved us on to follow him, and we did.

There were a lot of us: correspondents and contributors and field producers and writers and executive producers and Jon. It took a long time for us to file onto the stage, and by the time we were all gathered up there, our walk-up music had long since ended. Our good shoes clopped hollowly on the stage as we assembled ourselves around Jon, and that's when I noticed: the applause had ended, too. It was a reminder that even for the most rightly famous and beloved and accomplished, there's only so much clapping before it's over. Especially at the Emmys, where you really need to move it along and get to the parties.

Jon rescued the moment, of course. "Without the music it

really feels very judgmental!" he said. "*It's been ten seconds,*" he said, channeling the audience's unspoken mind. "*Entertain us!*"

And that's how he won them back and said the rest of whatever words he said. You can find them on YouTube, just like I did. I couldn't have remembered any of them otherwise. I wish I could tell you what it felt like to look out from that stage into that huge audience, into the millions of eyes behind the camera lenses, but I don't remember that either, because I was standing in the back.

What I could see were my friends' backs and shoulders. Unlike them, I was always freelance. I would stroll in for a few days every third week or so, hang around and write and eat a free lunch and then get dressed up in a suit or a *Tron* outfit or whatever they wanted me to wear. I would say my words and make my faces and then go home. I was never there day to day, every day, making the show run. So I nestled myself in the background, near LL Cool J (another interloper), where I belonged.

I did not expect to get emotional remembering this part. Until now, I just remembered it as a good night, a grace-note premise to get to the next part of the story, the part with the Property Brothers. But here I am writing this moment, and I am stuck in it, almost crying.

I looked at the backs and shoulders of my friends, and I loved those backs and shoulders. I had entered the *Daily Show* office almost exactly ten years earlier with no television experience, a true impostor, and they had welcomed and encouraged me and taught me. After a while I felt less like an impostor because of their faith and, frankly, their training, the inspiration of their intense competence, and the merciless deadline of 4 p.m. rehearsal, day after day. (It really is an almost *daily* show!) And now it was over.

Jon's final show had been a few weeks before. We had all said our good-byes. But we had known then that they were fake good-byes, because we would be back together, one more time, at least, on this fancy field trip to the Emmys. But now, as Jon was wrapping up his words, this was over too. What makes me almost cry is feeling the nearness of those backs and shoulders, and knowing that nearness would soon end.

"Thank you so very much," Jon said finally to the audience. "You will never have to see me again."

We were ushered offstage. As we stepped behind the curtain, LL Cool J touched my shoulder.

"Congratulations," LL Cool J said to *me*, of all people, which made about as much sense as anything.

"Thank you, LL Cool J," I said.

They brought us to a backstage celebrity lounge. What was obviously, at its bones, a bare multipurpose room had been transformed into a moody, plush, fake hotel lobby. It was full of sofas and throw pillows and french fries—bags and bags of McDonald's fries, arrayed on a huge table.

Someone explained that we would go into the next room shortly to take questions from the press, but in the meantime, please enjoy these french fries from McDonald's. I noticed that whenever any one of my famous friends ate a french fry, someone from the McDonald's social media team would try to secretly take their picture.

Then we were brought into another room. This other bare multipurpose room had not been transformed at all. The light was bright and harsh, and there were no sofas or fries, just dozens of cruddy folding chairs full of reporters, who were non-famous and therefore non-human.

We gathered around Jon in front of a black scrim as he took some questions. Many of them were about Donald Trump, who was running for president at the time. Do you remember that? How there was a time before this time? When we thought we understood what politics was, what entertainment was, and what the difference was between them?

The reporters asked if Donald Trump running for office meant the end of satire. Jon said no. They asked if Donald Trump were elected president, would Jon come back to television? Jon said absolutely not.

I understood how Jon felt, or at least I knew how *I* felt. A few years earlier I had changed my persona on *The Daily Show* from the "Resident Expert" to the "Deranged Millionaire." I did this in large part to make fun of Donald Trump. Because even back then, Donald Trump was appearing on cable news channels to peddle conspiracy theories about Barack Obama's religion and place of birth. It was 2011. *The Apprentice* was winding down and struggling. Like anyone, Donald Trump wanted to stay on television, so he was trying out some new ways of doing so, such as musing about running for president and/or just wandering onto cable news sets to tell obvious lies without any credentials other than that he was a (supposedly) rich white man who wanted to talk right now. I told *The Daily Show* that we should have our own entitled, wealthy, lunatic white male monster, and that person should be me, and they agreed with me.

That bought me several years of happy work, but I very quickly learned I had made a mistake. My comedy, such as it is, had always been based on taking existing fact and stretching it out to its most absurd possible iteration. But Donald Trump was already doing that. He had been doing it his whole life. By the time he launched his actual, no-joke presidential campaign by gliding down a golden escalator to accuse Mexico of rape, I had realized that there was no joke I could make that could keep up with the long-form improv Trump was laying down every hour of every day. Because of course we now know the no-joke campaign *was* a joke. He never expected to actually be elected. He just wanted to launch this new, lucrative hate-and-fear-based entertainment product called the Trump Candidacy. But then he became president, and the joke was on him, because he did not want that job. But the joke was still mostly on us, because he is terrible at it, and he makes us all a laughingstock.

A running question I recall from my time on *The Daily Show* came from columnists and pundits musing, why is there no right-wing *Daily Show*? And we would glibly, pridefully answer that the conservative movement could not be funny because it was, by nature, authoritarian, prudish, untruthful, and dull. This was a comforting lie. Now we know that Trump *was* the right-wing *Daily Show* all along, but in a highly sophisticated form we smarty-pants never expected. We never expected the right-wing *Daily Show* was going to be Andy Kaufman. We didn't expect it to be a single, intensely weird and ultimately unknowable performance artist who would never break character. And he would not have his own television show, but hijack *all* the television shows as well as *all* those new streams and apps and formats and platforms we didn't understand, all to force his disruptive, meta, upsetting anti-comedy on us from every side of culture, making us live in a MAGA-themed *Sleep No More* immersive experience the size and shape of the whole country.

I didn't understand all of that then, at the Emmys. All I knew was that Donald Trump was better than me at Donald Trump jokes, so I had ended up locking myself into a few years on the show doing generic financial services comedy for which I could not be less qualified. So when Trevor Noah asked if I wanted to consider staying on the show, I finally said no thank you.

But now you are wondering why I am talking about *me* so much when I earlier had mentioned the Property Brothers. *We don't want* you, you are thinking. Along with every other human on earth, including myself, you are thinking, *we want those Prop Bros!*

So yes, but we have to back up a bit in the story to find them.

Because there was no moment at my last Emmys where the change in culture had become more obvious to me than before the ceremony even began. After many visits to the Emmys, I knew to avoid the crush of tuxedos and cocktail dresses trying to push their way in the main doors of the auditorium, and instead slip forward easily down the house-right hallway and enter the theater at the foot of the stage. Then you walk by the front rows, where all the most famous people sit, and find your way back to your seat. This year, I scanned my ticket and saw that *The Daily Show* was seated pretty far back, house left. As I was crossing over I heard twin voices. "Hey, John!" they said. "Hey, John!"

It was Jonathan Scott and Drew Scott, aka the Property Brothers. I do not need to tell you who the Property Brothers are. I realize that now. But just in case you don't know, they are two very nice and friendly identical Canadian twins who renovate and sell homes on TV. I had met them on Twitter, and it is always my great thrill to admit that I know them a little bit and that they are nice to me. But I did not expect to see them here at the Emmys, dead center in the third row, smiling, one in a cream dinner jacket, the other in a green tuxedo. (They do not dress alike. They know what they're doing.)

"Hey, John!" they called.

"It's the Property Brothers!" I called back.

"Are you here with *The Daily Show*?" they asked.

"Yes," I said. "What are *you* doing here?"

I knew they had been nominated for Best Structured Reality

Show, but that had been awarded the previous weekend, along with a lot of the technical awards the Academy relegates to the junior prom–ish "Creative Arts" Emmys. I also knew they had not won their category.

"Are you presenting an award?" I asked.

"No," they said. "They just invited us!"

"Oh," I said. I had clearly misunderstood just how famous the Property Brothers were. I had thought they were just nice guys on Twitter with a little reality show, until my daughter told me how dumb I was. Now they were front and center, while Jon Stewart, the liberal conscience of cable television for sixteen years, had been exiled to the distant weeds of far house left, along with the likes of me. The Prop Bros had no purpose here, no job other than to sit third-row center and glow in the light of the stage. That's just where the Emmys wanted them.

"OK," I said. "I'll see you later." And I started my walk back to the *Daily Show* seats. I walked and I walked and I walked, until Jonathan and Drew were just likable cream and green specks near the stage.

After the whole ceremony was finally over, everyone in the theater trooped over to the Los Angeles Convention Center for the Governors Ball. Once again a grim, functional space was draped in velvet and fairy lights. Andrea Bocelli sang from atop a tall, rotating circular stage, but it was the Property Brothers who were the center of attention. Everyone wanted to hang with Jonathan and Drew Property. People tittered and high-fived in their wake as they walked through the room.

Tina Fey and Kristen Schaal got selfies with them, and at some point I saw Jon Hamm making out with both of them. (Ha ha, just kidding, Hammy. Just making sure you're reading.) They were genuinely nice and happy to be there, like a pair of famous corgis (but with actual real estate chops), and I was reminded once again that genuine niceness and happiness are attractive to people.

At one point, Jonathan sat down at my table to talk. We took a photo together, and I felt my stock at the Governors Ball instantly rise. After he left, people asked me, "Do you know them? Can you introduce me?" I didn't mind. I would rather be famous for knowing a Property Brother a little than not be famous at all.

A few weeks later, Jonathan called me. They were producing some reality television shows, and he wanted to know if I wanted to be a part of it. He told me one idea, in which I would lead the audience into secret rooms and chambers all over the world. This was my dream job, of course. It is, essentially, what this whole book is all about.

But Jonathan Property knew what my dream job was before even I did. And even though I now understood how famous and savvy they were, and even though Jonathan was offering to lead me from the past into the future of whatever entertainment was, I was not ready to do a reality show yet. Like the Emmys in 2008, I was still a snob. I said no thank you. He was very very very nice about it. He always is.

I knew the moment I hung up that I had made a terrible

mistake. But then, almost immediately, I was offered another golden opportunity from Canada. A man emailed me from Toronto asking if I would come to his girlfriend's birthday party. I wouldn't have to do anything at the party. His girlfriend was just a big fan, and he was just a Canadian millionaire who wanted to make her happy. He said he would pay me twenty-two thousand American dollars.

I was very torn. I had turned down my dream job of going into secret rooms on television and had nothing else really going on. And this was a lot of money. But I still didn't want to do it. I said to my wife, "I don't want to be purchased for someone's girlfriend. I don't want to jump out of a cake."

She said, "You should do it, though."

She was right. As always, it is better to say yes than no. *I* don't know what entertainment is anymore, so maybe I should find out. Maybe this would be my *new* dream job, my new, genre-defying, Trumpian art form of being a corgi at a party. So I told my agent I would do it, but only if the Canadian millionaire paid me fifty thousand dollars, and *only* if I got to jump out of an actual cake. My agent passed along my two conditions.

I don't know which is the better way to end this story. To tell you that the Canadian millionaire immediately said yes? Or to tell you that "yes" was the last thing he said? Because after that, he stopped writing back. The party never happened, and after some investigation on my agent's part, it was revealed that the Canadian millionaire, if he really was either of those things, had just been playing a joke on me. I was part of *his* new art form. Maybe, in an apartment somewhere in Toronto, he has my emails framed on the wall, along with emails from all the other somewhat famous people he's tricked. Maybe he brings in strangers to see what John Hodgman was willing to do for money. Too bad for him. I would have been great jumping out of that cake.

Meanwhile, Property Brothers, if you're reading this, hello! Thank you again, Drew, for inviting me to your and Linda's wedding in Italy. It was great to see you there too, Jonathan. I was serious when I said I am ready to do a reality show now. Specifically I am suggesting a show called *Property Only Child*, where I go with young, childless couples and help them pick out their dream home in Winnipeg or whatever, and then I ask if I can then live with them as their very special boy. Think it over.

Chapter Thirteen

A GREAT WAY TO RUIN A DIAMOND

I was still only Platinum when I learned the television show had been canceled. I met the news with the same mix of relief and disappointment that I suspect I would have felt if the show had been renewed for another year. But now *The Daily Show* was over for me as well, and I was facing the new reality that I was not on television at all, and I did not know if I ever would be again.

Television was always an accident in my life. I never expected it to last, at least not until it lasted *just* long enough that I got tricked into thinking it was never going to end. I could finally be with my family, and all of them were healthy, and we had many things to feel lucky about. But endings are hard, even (and especially) if you see them coming.

So I was up at 2 a.m. one night, mournfully thinking about this at the kitchen counter, when I got an email. It explained to me that I had a chance to raise my Medallion Status even higher. I was, in fact, only seven thousand MQMs shy of going *Diamond*.

You may wonder, what is the difference between Diamond Medallion status and Platinum Medallion status? Again, here in the thin upper atmosphere of the Medallion program, the differences are minor. I mentioned the Sky Lounge membership earlier. With Diamond you can also board with first class no matter where you are seated, but again you have to wait for the pre-boarders and the liars who slip into their ranks. And supposedly you are super-DUPER eligible for automatic upgrades, but again: this is mostly a fiction. One hears legends of people getting quietly bumped up to first class, moments before a flight. But it has never happened to me.

The main distinction of the Diamond Medallion is that in real life, you would never make a medallion out of a diamond. Silver, gold, even platinum medallions at least *exist*, theoretically. But diamonds are prized for the four Cs: clarity, color, carat, and cut. Creating the complex, symmetrical facets that bring the diamonds alive with deep, reflected light is an art form. Band-sawing one into a dumb, two-facet slab that can be hung on a ribbon is mostly just a great way to ruin a diamond.

But in cold December, approaching the year's longest night and a new, uncertain future, this stupidity only increased my yearning. All I knew, all I *needed* to know, was that there was an ugly, impossible, imaginary prize that someone *else* had, and I did not. And I was never going to get this chance again. If I earned those points before the end of December, I would be Diamond all of next year. But if I didn't, I would stay Platinum, because my show and all its attendant semi-fame and free travel were over. I could see my children now and be a part of their lives, but they could also see *me*, and would watch me dwindle back to Gold, eventually to Silver, and then to nothingness.

I opened my computer and began checking flights. There was nowhere I needed to go, but I knew I would need to go at least across the country, and I had very little time in which to make the trip, as we were about to slam right up into the holidays. Finally I calculated that the only option was for me to fly cross country, to Los Angeles, say, early on a Sunday morning, to stay there for a couple of hours and then catch a red-eye flight directly back home. And there was no choice: I would have to fly first class. Even premium economy would not earn me the MQMs I needed to go Diamond and make the whole pointless trip slightly less pointless. I chose my seat and priced it out. It was going to cost $3,500.

I thought for a long time at 2 a.m. about this. I now know that there is a special Beloved website you can go to just to throw your money at the airline so they will up your status without you having to travel, but it may not have existed then, and anyway I didn't know that at the time. I also now know that people who, like me, become addicted to loyalty programs employ all kinds of tactics to maximize miles. They "churn" credit cards, applying for multiple airline-cobranded credit cards, soaking up the on-signing mileage bonuses, spending thousands in the first few months to trigger new bonuses, then canceling the cards, waiting a period, and signing up again.

In 1999, an engineer named David Phillips noticed that the Healthy Choice brand of arguably healthy packaged foods was offering one hundred miles to be applied to a loyalty program of your choice for every Healthy Choice UPC code returned to them in the month of May. Phillips spent $3,214 to pack his garage full of 12,150 Healthy Choice pudding cups, and, trading the pudding inside for free label peeling from local Salvation Army volunteers, ultimately earned one and a quarter million miles and lifetime AAdvantage Gold status with American Airlines. (I had to hire someone to type in those last letters, as words pertaining to non-Beloved status programs just look like nonsense symbols to me.)

And there are any number of websites and bulletin boards and even annual IRL conferences where points-chasers gather to discuss their latest mileage runs. Mileage runs are destinationless journeys, routes, some short- and some long-haul that have been stress-tested for maximum mile return for minimum cash investment. Humans like doing this, and some humans like getting other humans to do it for them. Steve Belkin is one of them. In 2001, he hired unemployed rice farmers to take four daily trips between two northern Thai cities at eight dollars a pop. In 1999, he earned 10.5 million miles hiring forty acquaintances to fly back and forth between Las Vegas and Los Angeles for two months.

But the difference between these extreme measures and my own was that these people were having fun. They were gaming the system, taking pleasure in finding flaws and loopholes and developing ingenious paths through and around them. They were not desperate addicts like me, about to throw full-price money at a problem that did not exist anywhere but in my mind.

The waste involved in this trip was obscene: of money, of jet fuel, of time. None of it was justifiable. Was I really going to do this? Fly five hours across the country? Get out at LAX? Leave the airport just long enough to go to the In-N-Out Burger that's right near the airport on Sepulveda? Was I going to have a double-double animal-style while sitting outside, watching those big planes land just across the road, roaring in-n-out of the sky and blasting your face with their diesel majesty, their liveries from around the world? Was I really not going to call anyone in LA, but be there, briefly, a lonely ghost without friends or family? And was I then going to just go back to the airport, reenter with no luggage one last time through that Beloved One portal, to take my seat on the plane and fly back through the night, eating first class food curated by Danny Meyer and drinking free whiskey and watching *Mad Max: Fury Road* three times?

As I considered it, I realized: this sounded like it was going to be the best day of my life.

But then I thought about my son. I thought about what he would say when I told him I could not bring him to school that morning.

"Are you going away again, Dada?" he would ask.

"Yes," I would reply.

"For work?" he would ask.

"Well . . ." I would reply. "It's hard to explain, son. I *have* to

---

leave you. I have to fly across the country, and I may need to use some of your college savings to pay for it. But don't worry: I will be flying right back. I just have to be there for a couple of hours. I just have to go to collect an imaginary medallion. But you understand, of course. You're a gamer. It's time for me to level up.

"Think of Pac-Man. Out there in the maze, there is a power dot. And if I go to Los Angeles and eat it, then for a brief moment, I will be bigger. For a brief period of time I will be able to turn around and eat the ghosts of guilt and doubt and shame and self-hatred (aka Shadow, Speedy, Bashful, and fucking Clyde), and as I eat them, the ghosts will say, 'Thank you for being Diamond on Beloved Airlines,' and I will leave briefly without constant fear. Because I will BE LOVED."

"Dada," my son might say. "I still do not understand. Why are you making a Pac-Man reference? I am only ten years old. Even if I understood your metaphor, you don't level up by eating a power dot, but by clearing the screen. And wouldn't a Diamond Medallion be more like a bonus prize, a bouncing bunch of cherries?"

"Son," I would say, "life is messy. Sometimes you just have to use a metaphor that makes its point, even if it's not perfect. Just like sometimes we have to do things that hurt other people. We know it is wrong and we are doing it anyway. And when that happens, we will mix any metaphor we have to to justify our actions and get out the door. You'll understand when you're disappointing your own children someday."

It was 3 a.m. now in my kitchen, the light barely chasing

away the deep night dark in the corners. The flight had been chosen. My passenger info and known traveler number and credit card security code had been entered. My finger touched the trackpad, guiding the pointer that hovered over the "Confirm and Buy" button. I waited. I made my decision.

Chapter Fourteen

THIS WAS ALL OPTIONAL

Around this time my cat, Petey, passed away. He was eighteen years old. I say "passed away," but what I mean is I paid a person to poison him. Don't worry, it was a veterinarian. Not a hobbyist. I'm not a complete monster.

I hope his life was happy, but I cannot know for sure, because he didn't often *seem* happy. Mostly he seemed mad, and he was kind of an asshole. I found him when he was about one year old, and even then, when he was young, he would not so much meow as *yell*, over and over again. Sometimes he was yelling for food. Sometimes he was yelling just for fun. He would slam his body into closed doors that he did not like being closed, and in the morning, he would walk on your face with litterbox paws. I loved him.

Eighteen years is a long time for a cat to be alive. By the end he was skeletal. He looked like he should be hosting a late-night anthology horror television show. He would walk around aimlessly yelling at ghosts, and seemed only to live on a single daily kibble and dust motes in shafts of sunlight.

My family and I were at the Popeyes in the Detroit airport. In fact, we were on our way back from Disneyland, now waiting on a connecting flight to Maine, when our cat sitter in Brooklyn called to tell us that Petey couldn't stand up anymore. I was not surprised. He had been getting weaker, and I figured this might happen. I asked her to take him over to the vet so they could board him for the night and keep an eye on him. I would find a flight back to Brooklyn and see what the situation was in the morning. I hung up.

I looked at my red beans and rice. I always enjoyed Popeyes red beans and rice because it tastes like eating spicy lard, and for the same reason, I didn't order it very often. The last time I had it was years before, and my phone rang then too. I was at the I-95 service plaza in Kennebunk, Maine, taking a break as we drove north to our Unnamed Coastal Town. I answered the phone. The man on the other end was a stranger. He told me my Social Security number. He told me he had stolen my identity and wanted me to give him money. Don't worry. It all worked out. I didn't pay him any money and so far I have not had my bank accounts cleaned out or been framed for murder. I'm not superstitious. I don't believe in magic beans, but now, in Detroit, I decided: I'm not going to eat those red beans and rice again. I don't need emotional trauma on top of my digestive trauma.

I found a flight to New York leaving in an hour. It was

departing just two gates away from our flight to Maine. I saw my wife and children off at the top of their jet bridge and walked, dazed, to my own new jet bridge and down to the plane. Maybe they thanked me for being Gold when they scanned my new boarding card. I don't remember.

As I flew home, I still wasn't totally sure that this wasn't just a false alarm. Petey had gone through a thing like this not long before. He suddenly could barely walk one day. We put him in the bathtub with a towel, a litter pan on one end, a food bowl on the other. We helped him navigate between them. And then after a few days, he shook it off and hopped out. For all I know he had died then and just didn't notice. For all I knew, he was unkillable, as he was already undead.

So when I got to the veterinarian's office, I expected her to suggest an expensive series of procedures and a pointless course of medications. But when I said Petey's name, she said, "Oh yes. Come with me."

She led me downstairs. I had never been downstairs. She brought me to an exam room. I had never been in this exam room. It was nicer than any of the others.

"This is a nice room," I said.

She said she would be back with Petey soon.

It *was* a nice room. The black upholstered armchair was nicer than the rickety stool I normally had to sit on. There was tasteful track lighting instead of fluorescents, and they warmed the somber, cream-white walls. What was that finish on those light fixtures? Oiled bronze? Very nice. But why were there so many Kleenex boxes around? What were these framed bits of comforting poetry on the wall? That tin-relief sculpture of a dog with wings?

And only then did I realize: *Oh. They have taken me to the killing room.*

The vet came in with Petey. He was sad and scared and not yelling. He was always smart, but I do not think he knew what was coming. Only I suddenly did. *My poor guy,* I said or thought. *My poor guy.*

I had found Petey on the street when I was twenty-six. He was standing by the garbage cans outside the neighboring apartment building. Just yelling and starving and obviously lost. He had no collar. I looked around for clues or help. There weren't any.

An old woman walked by. "Oh, he's a good cat," she said. "You should take him in." I didn't know how or if she knew him, but something in her advice felt like a spell in fable. I picked him up and he scratched the hell out of me. I put him in my studio apartment, brought him food and litter, and then went to work.

I posted "Lost Cat" signs with his picture, but no one wanted to claim him. I do not know how he had become lost. But I had to guess that he had been out there eating garbage and rats for some time, because when he used the litterbox, my studio apartment would fill instantly with a deep graveyard smell of rank decay. It was so strong a smell, it would wake me from a dead sleep, and then I would hear him scratching, scratching, burying his shame in the dark, and then he would yell for a while.

This is why no one claimed him, I thought. *Maybe that old woman had taken him in, but the smell and the noise was so bad that she placed him outside that morning, looking for someone to pass this curse on to, and that was me. And now it is my job to live in this smell for who knows how many years. Seventeen? Seventeen whole years living trapped with him in a toxic cloud of poop smell and constant, loud need.*

But as his system got cleaned out, the smell abated. I named him Petey, after Albert Brooks's pet bird in *Modern Romance*, and he was mine.

It was an accident that I had a cat, but I was open to it. Single people get pets in their twenties because it feels like a grown-up thing to do. You have a job now. Maybe you have an apartment of your own, or a room in one, that you can fill with your grown-up idea of art and music. You don't have money, but you learn to roast a chicken and invite your broke friends around your rickety side table for a fake grown-up dinner, pouring wine and mashed potatoes on top of your fear that you don't know what you're doing and never will. And you get a pet. You don't have to ask your mom and dad for one anymore. You can get that puppy or that kitten or that reticulated python you always wanted. It's liberating! And you kind of want to see if you are ready to care about a creature that is not you, and cannot give you a job or have sex with you.

Single people who *don't* get pets in their twenties have to do *other* things to pretend they are grown-ups, like get married. This is usually a terrible idea—about as bad as getting a reticulated python. Yes, it's fun to walk around on a spring day through the park holding hands with your new spouse, your grown-up love draped magnificently over your shoulders like an exotic snake. You get a lot of attention and feel cool. But you are also taking a huge, powerful thing into your life that requires an extraordinary amount of care and work and ugly sacrifice. You don't need to feed your marriage rodents. You don't have to kill a rat and then watch as your marriage slowly chokes it down. But marriage offers its own David Cronenbergian body horrors. It's not all fun hugging and kissing. You are sleeping and farting and snorting and flaking and puking in close proximity, and there is no way to hide all of these sounds and smells from your beloved. You see your partner unhinge their jaw to say the worst things, or shed their disgusting skin to become something new, and you have to accept and forgive these things. A marriage, like a python, is expensive. It gets bigger and bigger and if you don't care for it, and if it dies, you have a big fucking problem on your hands. Quick: Do you know what to do when you come home to find that you have a dead twenty-foot python stuck behind the radiator of your grown-up married apartment? Or decaying in the walls? I don't. But I bet whatever you have to do, it's probably easier than getting a divorce.

But sometimes people get married for better reasons than to prove they are grown-ups. And sometimes, if they do not already have pets, they will get one. Usually they get a puppy. They do not necessarily know that they are doing this to test their ability to keep a hilariously happy and stupid creature alive. They don't know that they are testing their emotional threshold for handling that other creature's feces. They don't know yet that this is a rehearsal baby.

For most married people who get puppies, it's great. You discover that it is really fun to be adored and wanted all the time, unconditionally. It is fun having complete control over another creature's life, dressing them up in amusing ways, taking them wherever you want to without asking them, and putting pictures of them on Instagram without their consent to get attention for yourself. It is not long before you think: *This is amazing!* You will think, *Here's an idea I just had out of the blue: maybe I will have children!* And then you get instantly pregnant and have a baby and forget about that puppy for the rest of your and its life.

This sounds harsh, but it's fine! Babies are more important than dogs (sorry, fur parents), and if you have a dog, it really doesn't matter because they are dumb. They are just so glad to have another floppy, hapless smell-generator in the pack. They want to protect that baby and they want to do it by covering it in saliva.

But cats are *not* dumb, perpetual infants. Cats require no pack. As far as cats are concerned, you were always on the bubble of acceptability to begin with. Don't get me wrong. Cats are capable of love. They love certain areas of your home at certain sunny times of the day. They love the soft toy that they pretend is a thing they killed. They love whatever invisible thing in the middle distance they are constantly staring and narrowing their eyes at. They are definitely in love with the warmth of your body, and they may even be somewhat fond of *you*. You love them, and while I'm not sure cats *love* being loved, they definitely like-like it, and they aren't stupid. They know when they are being replaced in your affections.

Petey certainly knew the moment we brought our daughter home. We placed her on the floor in her car seat when we got home from the hospital. He sniffed her once, and then did not look at her again for nine years. He looked at me instead. I have never withered under such disappointed contempt. He didn't even yell. He just slunk away. Later, when the dried stump of our daughter's umbilical cord dropped off her body, he made it into his toy.

There is a reason for the old superstition that a cat will steal a baby's breath. *They want to do it*. And they *would* do it if they had the thumbs and paw strength to haul a Dustbuster up to the crib and turn it on.

But even if your cat is not into it, *you* at least are having fun with these babies, these new reflections of your ability to love. They exhaust you, and they also yell and run into doors, but unlike any pet, they are *of* you. And then, quicker than you think, they stop running into doors. Suddenly you are lying on the floor with your daughter, listening to the radio in the middle of the day, trying to let half your brain sleep while the other half concentrates on not letting her creep into the dustworld under the dresser, and she is levitating. Her body is lifting itself on its own feet for the first time, and the world disappears as you watch the surprise and pride crossing her face. Nothing exists beyond her in that moment, not your cat, not the fact that Bruce Campbell is on *Fresh Air*. For a moment, even *you* disappear, and you're surprised at what a relief it is.

Sooner than you think, your children stop yelling unshaped mouth sounds and start saying words. They say "I love you," and they are so convincing that you believe you maybe deserve it. And you pour that love back into them, as well as into your personal taste in books and music and television.

Also, you can dress them any way you like, but now you have the option of PANTS. So no wonder you stop taking pictures of your cat and start taking pictures of your child. No wonder the litterbox goes unchanged and the water bowl gets stale.

Eventually cats come around. They will appreciate that your children are also potential sources of heat and pets. But for a long time, the biggest role your cat will play in your child's life is as an opportunity for ethical instruction.

"Do not pull the cat's tail," you will say to your child. "If it is not fun for everyone, it is not fun for anyone."

"Do not touch the cat's bum," you will say. "It is dirty, and the cat cannot offer consent. Leave it alone."

"Fatty's bum," your child will reply charmingly. "Leave it."

Your child calls your cat Fatty. It does not care about your cat's feelings, and neither do you. It is not your pet anymore. It is an asshole who lives with you.

And then you have another child, and that paves the way for

the ultimate insult: a hamster. Soon your children take the hints the cat has been leaving for them (peeing on their pillows) and demand a new pet that *they* can love. So you get a dwarf hamster and name it Flurry, and your children are so happy and excited.

Your cat gets the message. *That's right*, you are saying to your cat. *We care more about this thing than you. And this thing is your food.*

But if cats could read English, I would tell them to take heart. Children don't actually like dwarf hamsters all *that* much. They are skittish prey animals. They have no tails to pull. And they don't just seethe when you pet them. When you pet a dwarf hamster, they bite you with needle teeth. And as you may recall from my book *Vacationland*, hamsters like Flurry don't linger on for eighteen years. They plump up quickly with strange tumors, or wither mysteriously from unknown ailments, and you alone are left to care for their failing bodies, because your children don't care about them, and also, your children don't care about you.

That last part is not wholly true. Of course your children love you. But they don't just stand up and learn to walk and then stop there. They *keep* growing and learning things. They don't *only* say, "I love you." Sometimes they don't say anything to you at all, because they are coming up with their own private thoughts and feelings and plans. They push you out of their lives and go places, both emotionally and, later, physically, where you cannot dress, photograph, see, or protect them, and nor should you try. They are not your pets either.

And that is when your cat takes his revenge. That is when he turns to you and says, *I'm still here.* He reminds you of the day you found him, when you were twenty-six, living in a studio apartment, just three doors down from the cool independent video store, and every night you could just stay up late and watch movies and answer to no one, a grown-up alone in the world. He reminds you that everything after that moment was *optional.* You could have remained the same selfish creep you were trying so hard to un-become, just getting money and having sex, or, if you were me, getting drunk in bars and arguing about operating systems. You didn't *have* to get a cat. You didn't *have* to have children. You didn't have to devote every minute, the life energy of your every cell, to worry, to the harried art of keeping something else alive. You didn't have to learn what it is like when you fail at that task.

The cat doesn't really say this. Cats can't talk. But for a rickety, declining year, he sends you the message: *We are both old. See how I cannot walk correctly or bathe myself? That's going to be* you *someday. Go ahead. Tell your kids about how we all decay and die. I will wait over here in the bathtub in a pool of my own urine.*

And then you are in a mournful room in the basement of a veterinarian's office, and you are about to pay someone to poison your pet. And the vet says, "You don't have to make this decision now. We could wait a few days and see if he improves."

And you are forced to say, "No. I have to get back to my family. This is the most convenient time for me to have him poisoned." And you know you are a monster after all, a sick animal that no one has the decency to put down.

That was how I felt at the time Petey died. But as I write this now, my children are even older than they were then, and further from my reach. Soon they will be gone altogether from my daily life. Petey's revenge was not to remind me that all this pain was optional. Because it becomes self-evident to any parent that the pain of loving and caring for another thing is better than the ease of not. I will admit even fur parents know this secret. Parenthood begins as an expression of narcissism, of personal genetic redoubling; but that selfishness is quickly burned away in the crucible of tears, vomit, fevers, and close calls; and it is repaid only in the incalculable joy of seeing someone else thrive in happiness and apart from you. You disappear, and it is a fucking relief.

Petey's revenge was to remind me that the creatures we raise and grow with, and disappear into, also grow and go away. And I was grateful to him. We need assholes in our lives to tell us the hard, true things we don't want to hear. That's why children become teenagers.

The vet told me I could say good-bye while Petey was still alive. I didn't have to be there as his breath slowed and stopped. But I was. I put my face into his fur. All the cells in our bodies had been replaced several times over since we first met. He was eighteen. He wasn't my pet anymore.

Chapter Fifteen

TIPS TO ACE YOUR AUDITION

For a while I actively tried to get back on television. I was going out for a lot of small television roles, and I grew to really love the exquisite humiliation of auditioning. When you audition for a role, everything is organized around reminding you that you do not matter. It's the best therapy I ever received.

You are told to report to an almost empty room in a grim office building at a time that is inconvenient to you. Usually there is no one there: just a few chairs and a table with a sheet of paper on it. You write your name on the sheet of paper and then sit down. You wait a long time. A light flickers. You wonder if you are being pranked. Then a young person will emerge from a blank door in the corridor and look at the piece of paper and say your name into the middle distance. "John?" they will say, as if half seeing a ghost in the corner. Because that is what you are to them.

"Yes," you will say. And then they take you through the blank door into the room.

This is if you are lucky. If you are unlucky, there are other people in the room, other ghosts auditioning for the same role. Sometimes you know them and you both have to pretend that you are not competing for the same job. Sometimes they are more famous than you are, people you see on television all the time. You stare at them wondering why *they* still have to audition. It reminds you that the acting profession itself is precisely and endlessly *this*: waiting in a room for your name to be called. And then you hear your name, and they take you through the blank door into the room.

The room has gray nubbly carpet and an empty wall that you stand in front of and a tripod with a camera on it. You are asked to attach a microphone to your shirt and say your name and height and weight. You feel like you are telling your family you are still alive after you have been taken hostage.

After you say your lines into the camera, sometimes the person in the room is encouraging. Sometimes they suggest you try it again, and that is when you know you've failed. But mostly their eyes are distant and inscrutable. I took this as kindness. They don't want you to get your hopes up. If you grew up, as I did, confusing praise with oxygen, the audition room is the utter vacuum of deepest space. But you can survive there. That was a remarkable lesson in itself. And the longer you spend in that praiseless void, the less you rely on it. This is called, I have read, "not giving a fuck," and it's very liberating!

One time I was asked to audition for a play. The character I was auditioning for was in a hospital, tending to his sick mother. He has a conversation with the main character in the play and recalls taking care of his adopted baby, who is now older, and then he cries. Crying on command and kissing some random other actor convincingly were two things I had never done (kissing Zach Galifianakis in *Bored to Death* doesn't count, because our lips were insulated by inches of thick mustache bramble), and I was terrified.

When preparing for an audition, I like to print out the script pages and walk around my neighborhood in Brooklyn. I check the pages as I run my lines, over and over, under my breath. Eventually I stop checking my pages and just walk around muttering to myself and making faces. This has the double benefit of training my memory and discouraging my neighbors from talking to me.

There were a lot of lines to learn for this audition before I even got to the crying part. I didn't think I could do it. They say that you should try to recall a time in your life when you were very sad and had cried before, but I didn't have much to offer. I mean, my own mother actually died, but weeks passed before I cried for *her*. And even that was not "crying" so much as it was a yelling series of dry heaves of anger and sorrow that lasted maybe four minutes and then went away. Everything in my body hurt, but my eyes were dry. The other time was when I saw *E.T.* with Tim McGonagle in 1982, and even then I just got a little misty before I froze up. That was it. Happy tears were also absent in my experience. I didn't cry at my wedding or the birth of my own children, nothing. My inability to cry, or at least to cry the way actors cry in movies, had in fact formed the basis of a long-held childhood theory I came up with to explain my own weirdness: *Maybe I am an android*, I would think. I was pretty excited about it, actually. But then I saw *Blade Runner*, and it turns out androids cry all the time. Roy Batty at the end bawling his eyes out about all the things he's seen: what a sap.

But then I finally got to the crying part of the script. And guess what? *It was easy.* Something had changed in me. Somehow it took no effort at all to burst into sobbing tears talking about taking care of a baby in the middle of a Park Slope street where I used to push my own babies in strollers but don't anymore. *Who knows what I could have connected to in that scene?* But it worked. I cried, and then walked some more. I went back to the beginning of my lines, and cried again. I cried all over the neighborhood. People would approach me and then think better of it, veering off to give me my space. It was great.

I went into the audition. At first I worried that I would get nervous and freeze up. But nope: I cried all over their faces. I was like Bruce Banner in *The Avengers* when he reveals he can turn into the Hulk at will: my secret is, I'm always crying.

I wanted to write just now how I wished the Director from my television show could have seen me. That would have tied this little story into the larger narrative of this book, but it would be false. I didn't care what she, or anyone, thought. For once.

The woman who wrote the play was there. "Are you OK?" she asked.

"I'm fantastic!" I said. "Thank you."

I was not even disappointed when I learned they gave the part to another person. He's a better actor for sure. But it was still my best audition, and I just wanted to tell you about it.

Chapter Sixteen

A PARABLE

One time I was flown on a private jet to a secret meeting. It was the same annual secret meeting where Neil Armstrong felt he didn't belong. After some years, I had finally been invited, and I *definitely* did not belong. I have never walked on the moon. I have barely walked on the earth, so faint shall the footprint of my life be upon this globe when I am gone. But I was invited and I said yes. And what I can tell you about flying in a private jet is: OF COURSE THEY DON'T MAKE YOU TURN YOUR PHONE OFF. Nobody cares. That's for nonfamous people.

This evening the secret meeting was held at a Masonic lodge. The Freemasons were not hosting it. They were just renting it to the secret meeting. They were renting it out because, contrary to what you may have heard on Alex Jones, the Freemasons do not rule the world. Maybe they did once. But now they need the money.

The room we assembled in was a beautiful theater. The

ceiling was painted like the twilight sky. Star-shaped lights il-luminated a golden carpet that sloped gently down to a fili-greed stage. I was told that here is where they staged their two-act allegory plays, steeping new initiates in the myth and allegory of the Masons' "peculiar system of morality."

I do not know the content of these plays. That's on pur-pose. It's a secret. But the Masons let us walk onstage and in-spect the scenic backdrops that would fly in as the allegory progressed: delicate, hand-painted scrims of sylvan woods and ancient temples. It was one of the most beautiful rooms I've ever been in.

Among the audience were famous actors, bestselling au-thors, fashion designers, and other public figures, and also a professional pickpocket. The pickpocket wore a spiffy pale gray three-piece suit and a sharp-brimmed hat. You know: pick-pocket garb.

He took turns calling people up from the audience and steal-ing their watches. He would just stand next to them and ask them friendly questions. "Did you have a good breakfast?" or "What was it like to star in that movie?" or "Did you like walk-ing on the moon?" That sort of thing.

They would answer the questions, smiling. They knew what was coming: their watch would be taken off their wrist. But they didn't know when it would happen.

And even when it happened, they didn't know. Some myste-rious movement occurred and then the pickpocket would just be casually dangling the watch over the subject's shoulder, out of his line of sight, and would keep asking questions as he went for the wallet.

Eventually the pickpocket would reveal that the famous successful person had been fleeced. The famous successful people would laugh about it. It was a morality play: a reminder that success does not mean you cannot be tricked.

Then one person was asked to come up. This person was a former government official. This person was a longtime public servant who was thoughtful and much smarter than I am. This person had peered into dark places, and probably saved lives, which is more than I can say.

Why was I even in that room? It's still a mystery to me.

But when you work at the high level this person worked at, lives are also lost. This person played a small but meaningful part in the launching of a disastrous war that was waged on false premises. To be fair, this person was not the architect of this war. They had just been given bad information. They had been tricked. This is not an excuse if someone you loved died in that war, but it's true.

But when this person was asked to come up and be tricked again, this person said no.

"Come on," said the pickpocket. "It's just fun."

This person shook their head. No. This person did not want to be tricked. This person did not want his or her watch stolen. This person did not want even this gentle, literal, slap on the wrist.

The pickpocket suggested that he had something else in

mind for this person and asked if this person would at least take a seat by the side of the stage while he stole one more watch. This person relented. The pickpocket stole another watch. Everyone had a good time.

Eventually the pickpocket turned back to the person who had been tricked into helping to start a war. The pickpocket mentioned that he noticed that person had taken his money out of his pocket.

"You saw that?" the person said.

"Yes," said the pickpocket. "You moved your money to your shoe. So I could not steal it."

The person revealed that this was so. The person tried to laugh. Maybe I'm wrong, but I did not see laughter in this person's eyes. I saw fury and terror.

Masons chose their ranks from among the leaders of their communities. But no matter their wealth, when they were initiated, they were blindfolded, either by a hood or a pair of hoodwinks. A noose was placed around their neck. Their chests were bared. Their status was removed from them.

They were ritually humiliated, and by passing through and surviving this shame, they were reminded that accomplishment and status do not equal virtue. Success does not make you smart enough not to be tricked.

But some people, I realized now, cannot surrender their status, even for a laugh in a secret meeting in a Masonic temple. For some people, status is what protects them from oblivion. And when they feel their status is slipping away from them, they act fearfully, irrationally. They do things like hide their money in their shoe, for example, or vote for Donald Trump.

However, if you think that is the full moral of the parable of the pickpocket, then you have missed the message of my arcane symbolism, dear initiate. READ ON.

Because after I observed this one exchange, I opened my eyes to the bigger picture. I didn't know why I was here, but I do know that very close to me there sat an extremely wealthy businessman, and over there was a former high-level government official, and there was the most famous actor in the world, and there was Neil Gaiman chatting with the ghost of Neil Armstrong. And we were all literally meeting, in *secret*, in an actual Masonic temple. Every conspiracy theory, it turns out, is absolutely true.

Chapter Seventeen

ALL I DO IS WIN

O nce I was no longer on television, I could spend more time with my son. He had started middle school, and the school was a few miles across Brooklyn near the Navy Yard. I knew this area: it was only a couple of blocks, in fact, from the studio where I used to pretend to be an evil FBI agent. There was a city bus that my son could take, but because I love him and hate the planet, I would frequently drive him to school in the morning.

It was good to spend time with him. We would talk and listen to music. I would play him "It's Tricky" by Run-DMC and explain how it was a response to those at the time who claimed that rapping was artless and easy. I would play him "King of Rock" and explain how that song started as a boast but became a prophecy. I would play him "Doesn't Make It Alright" by The Specials and explain how radical an interracial band was at that time, and how unfair it was that ska had become a punchline, while punk, which quickly devolved into a fashion pose for affluent suburban white dudes, remains revered. Yes. I was *that* dad, and I am confident my son enjoyed and appreciated every minute of these lectures.

But it wasn't a one-way street. My son played me his own songs and YouTubers and showed me his favorite all-Mormon sketch comedy troupe. They had all met and started performing comedy at Brigham Young University, but they stayed together after graduation and were now putting out two videos a week for their two million YouTube subscribers. They were wildly popular, and like all wildly popular things these days, no one had ever heard of them. I became obsessed with them. Their comedy studiously avoided curse words and innuendo and politics. This limited their subject matter somewhat. There were a lot of *Harry Potter* and *Star Wars* parodies and a series of sketches about lobster bisque. It was disorienting to experience comedy that was completely and earnestly free of subversion, critique, and anger. But they were funny, and the first lobster bisque sketch is a masterpiece. Mostly I envied their vigor and industriousness and good cheer, especially on mornings when I was hungover.

For a couple of weeks my son somehow got very deep into DJ Khaled, like the rest of America. During this time, he would play DJ Khaled almost every morning as we drove. If you are a screenwriter and you are looking for the perfect opening scene of your indie movie about middle age, just angle on a mid-forties white man with a beard and a Hartford Whalers hat, exhausted, bleary, not on television anymore, staring into the drizzle on his windshield at a stop light while his son blasts "All I Do Is Win."

(But please, screenwriters: Do not follow that scene with the dad dropping off his son and then idling in front of the gates of the studio where he used to pretend to be an evil FBI agent. Don't show the dad texting his friends inside the studio "I'm here if you need me," as a half joke that is no joke at all. That would be too much. That would be unsubtle… a little on the nose, as they say.)

I don't remember what we were listening to on the morning the other car hit us. It was not a serious collision. We were just rear-ended at a stoplight. I couldn't even blame the young woman who had hit us, because she had been rear-ended as well, pushed into my bumper by a dude who had pulled out and driven away. We looked at our cars and saw there was no damage. We were lucky, we agreed. But we were shaken up. My family and I had been in a good mood that morning. But even the smallest fender bender smashes your day and your nerves and sends them hurtling in a new direction. Even if you can drive away from the scene, as we did, your stomach feels lost behind your body, stuck at the scene of the accident, while your brain scans anxiously the alternate futures, all the dark timelines that you avoided by being so lucky. And you have to pretend it was no big deal. "We are lucky," you say. "It could have been much worse."

We arrived at school and had our days, and then that night Donald Trump was elected president.

———————

WE HAD ALL BEEN IN a good mood that morning. Before our car was hit, my son and I had gone with my wife and daughter to the local YMCA to vote. We were all excited at the prospect of electing the first woman president. It was an inevitability. As a straight white dude, I was especially ready to hand this world to my daughter and her generation. We had had a hell of a run, but it was time.

My daughter had always supported Hillary. The night before Election Day, she was calling voters in Florida. She got my wife to do it too. The Saturday before Election Day, she had gone to West Philadelphia with a friend and the friend's mom to knock on doors. She was fourteen. We were terrified to let her go. We were afraid she would get hurt. But she wasn't afraid.

(Not that I hadn't done MY PART to help, by the way. I did a bunch of tweets, after all. And also I wrote a blog post endorsing Hillary Clinton that I'm pretty sure caused both Henry Winkler and David Lynch to unfollow me. SO IT'S NOT LIKE I WASN'T TAKING RISKS AND MAKING SACRIFICES.)

The morning of Election Day, my daughter joined me behind the weird little blast-shield desk as I filled out my ballot. My daughter watched me as I filled out the little bubbles with the pen. Pride and happiness and hope shimmered off her. When it came time to fill in the bubble beside Hillary Clinton's name, I handed the ballot to her. She filled in the bubble. She was so so so careful to fill it in all the way.

———————

When it came time to put the ballot in the machine, however, a poll watcher approached us. "You let your daughter touch your ballot. That is election fraud." He took the ballot away from me and tore it up in our faces.

HA HA, that is not true. I scanned the ballot just fine, and joined the majority of humans in the USA who chose Hillary Clinton and the future over a bogus maybe-millionaire wizard daddy who said he was going to take us back to the '50s in his cardboard-box time machine.

And then we went about our day. My son and I got hit by a car, but it was fine. Everything was going to be fine. And then we came home and watched television. My son, who is younger, went to bed early, long before optimism turned rancid.

My daughter and wife and I stayed up just late enough to feel the impossible encroaching. It was my goal to become unconscious by any means while there was still a glimmer of surprise possible, somewhere, in some state out on the far side of 1 a.m. Through legal means well-honed over the years (gin and melatonin), I managed to do exactly that. But it was already too late: I had already watched the happiness fade from my daughter's face, watched it become paler as excitement was replaced with confusion, dread, shock. Tears came, the kind that come when someone or something dies, and you know it can't be taken back or fixed. Time breaks in half to *before* and *after*. Nothing will be the same.

"How could this happen?" she asked, before I went to bed. "How could this happen?"

It is no fun to have no answer for a child in mourning.

And in the morning, I got to tell my son what had happened, and there were more tears for all of us. But soon, for my daughter the tears were replaced by an ashen, sad understanding.

Whatever you may have thought about Hillary Clinton, my daughter watched as a highly experienced and qualified woman lost a job to a neophyte dilettante cartoon character of a white man who openly bragged of molesting women. My daughter isn't dumb. She got the message.

When my son and I drove to school that morning, we did not listen to "All I Do Is Win." Instead, we stared sadly and I told him about the five stages of grief: anger, bargaining, depression, acceptance. But first: denial.

After I dropped him off, I turned on the car radio. I listened for a bit to Donald Trump's remarks in which he extended warm compliments to the woman he had just yesterday promised to put in jail. I turned it off and pretended it wasn't happening. I wanted to buy a hat: "Make America November 7th Again."

NINE DAYS AFTER THE ELECTION I had a comedy show scheduled in Bethlehem, Pennsylvania. I did not feel like doing it. I was mad and sad and terrified to go there. I knew that this particular county had not voted for Trump, but it was surrounded by counties that had. Still, I knew other people felt the same way I did, and some of them had bought tickets to see me. So I slouched my way over there.

The comedy show was in an old steel plant that had been transformed into an arts venue. There are many performance spaces in the venue (steel plants are large). The stage I was standing on was backed by giant glass windows looking out over the massive steel furnaces, long ago shut down. The furnaces were bathed in colored lights from below.

I asked if anyone in the audience had voted for Trump. A man raised his hand. I wanted to say, "You are my fellow citizen and neighbor, but I'm going to need a minute with you, because you hurt my children."

But I couldn't get angry at this guy. He was in his fifties, a white guy with a lanky runner's body, wearing a salmon T-shirt or polo (can't remember). He looked like a happy high school chemistry teacher. He was probably just a lifelong Republican who wanted a tax break and held his nose, or someone who just hated Hillary Clinton *so much*. He was neither brave nor ashamed when he raised his hand, just affable, smiling, untouchable.

I couldn't get angry at him because he was a guest in my audience (why he was there was its own kind of disruptive mystery), just as I was a guest in his dead steel plant.

"I get it," I said. I pointed out that this plant used to employ ten thousand humans, each with a family. And now it is an arts center, and over there is a cocktail-and-craft-beer bar. Those furnaces behind me are cold. They're never coming back, no matter what anyone promises you. They used to make steel and prosperity here, but now they are my backdrop: a man from television and Massachusetts who has come here to make jokes about his two summer homes and tell you that you voted wrong. I get it. I get why it would be fun to hurt a person like me. I hate myself too.

But here we were, together anyway. I said, "I hope you enjoy the comedy." He seemed to. He stayed until the end.

Later I learned that another couple did walk out at some point. The server came back with their check and they were just gone. I don't know who they voted for, but they wanted to hurt me too, and instead they just hurt the blameless server who had brought them their nachos. It made about as much sense as voting for Donald fucking Trump. I was so angry.

A FEW WEEKS AFTER THE ELECTION, my heels began to hurt. Every step felt like I was impaling each foot onto a steel spike. I eventually went to a podiatrist. This was something I could do because I have health insurance, a flexible schedule, and the confidence that I will not be arrested and deported if I seek medical attention.

The podiatrist took X-rays of my feet and showed me the heel spur on my right foot and the developing one on my left. He explained that when there is a microtear in the fascia covering the heel, your dumb body sends bone there to "protect" the area. And because you are walking on your dumb feet all day long, you only prolong the injury, prompting your dumb body to send more bone stuff (medical term. Sorry. Try to keep up) down the leg, until your heel is protected by a sharp internal spike of hard, pointed-yet-pointless bone that you get to walk on every day.

He explained that the problem was my calves. The muscles in my calves were exceptionally tight, pulling on the fascia all night, causing the pain. Now this was hard to hear. I have always had flab, a weak chin, neck meat, and man boobs. But my legs, through no effort of my own, have always been beautiful marble pythons, and my calves especially are well-shaped and developed. People who see my calves gasp, and when you see me next, you will too. But now my calves had betrayed me.

The podiatrist cradled one in his hand. "Everything you are suffering comes from this exquisite tightness," he said.

My heel spurs were embarrassing for two reasons. First, given the timing, and given the fact that it was heel spurs that had kept Donald Trump from going to Vietnam, it was obvious that my body was hitting me with the most unsubtle, on-the-nose psychosomatic metaphor of all time. And second, because each step was a reminder: this small pain, this nuisance, this blunt metaphor was probably the worst I personally would have to deal with in the Trump era. I felt deep shame. I thought about the Trump voter in my audience in the former steel mill turned arts center. I'm sure he didn't mean for his vote to hurt me and my children. I'm sure he *meant* no harm to all the vulnerable communities of non-white male John Hodgmans that Trump openly targeted during his campaign. But harm is what they would be getting, right away and on purpose, and it's not heel spurs. The podiatrist offered to stick a long needle full of cortisone deep into my heel. It hurt a lot and helped very little, but I accepted it. It's what I deserved.

On the day after Trump's inauguration, my wife and daughter went to Washington, DC, to join the Women's March. My son and I joined the march in Manhattan.

At first we were not going to go. I wondered if the women really wanted two more white guys around right now. But mostly I just wanted to hide in the dark all the time. Going outside was no longer fun. We had just learned that we had wildly misjudged the direction of history, underestimated the fury of people we considered neighbors, and even New York felt like new, unknown territory.

The morning after the election, after I dropped my son off at school, I had driven into Manhattan. I had some voice-over work booked in a studio there, but I was early, so I stopped into Eisenberg's. Eisenberg's is a lunch counter on Fifth Avenue I had been going to since I moved to New York, though Eisenberg's has been there since 1929. I liked it because it was a hot, narrow place where people from all different backgrounds jammed themselves in next to each other to be yelled at by the counterman before he hurled home fries or tuna salad or egg creams or matzoh ball soup at you—all with a certain delicious Eisenbergian grease-gloss on them that you cannot get anyplace else on earth—and then, after a while, the counterman decided you were OK. He didn't *really* hate you and actually remembered your name. This used to be a metaphor for what all of New York was like, but more recently it felt like all that remains of *that* New York was Eisenberg's itself. I also liked Eisenberg's because they kept a photo of me on the wall along with other somewhat well-known New Yorkers. Every time I went in there, I would worry they had figured me out and thrown it in the trash, and every time I saw it hanging still, I could breathe again. I needed that comfort now.

Eisenberg's is normally a chatty place. But on the morning after the election, it was dead silent. It was impossible to tell who was shocked into silence and who was quietly glad at our shock. It was sad and exhausting. I was not used to making a threat assessment every time I walk into a room of strangers. (That's because I am not a woman.)

So yes, I was wary about going outside, and also I didn't want to go to the Women's March because my feet hurt so badly. But David Rees was going to the Women's March, and he told me I had to go too. David Rees is my friend and conscience. He has a moral bluntness that was echoed in his sign: a small piece of cardboard that read "Nazis Suck." So my son and I joined him and marched up Fifth Avenue.

It was January, but the day was bright and warm. It was good to be pressed in among everyone else who had been told they didn't understand their own country, that we were not the real Americans because we did not live in low-population states. It was good to feel like the sun could still shine on us, that we didn't just have to trudge forward in sickly gaslight. It was good to follow the women, and to see my son follow them and follow them in their chants. "This is what democracy looks like," my son repeated after them. It was good to see him happy. And it was good to remember that there are so many of us, in fact 2.9 million *more* of us, and that there are no good chants about the electoral college, because it's stupid.

It was joyous, but it was also sad. The inauguration was over. For weeks leading up to it, we had hoped something would stop it. We traded fantasies on Twitter: *I've heard the electoral college is going to go rogue. I've heard the Supreme Court is going to kidnap him. I've heard that all of the living former presidents are going to revolve the Washington Monument five times and reset the timeline, just like Hamilton wrote about in Secret Federalist #666. I've heard that Lawrence Lessig says that the 2000 election established a legal precedent to overturn the electoral college vote, which is great because once we have chucked Trump out, all of Trump's supporters are going to totally accept President Clinton's legitimacy because a Harvard professor told them it was legal. It would be like Trump never ever happened.*

"This is called bargaining," I had explained to my son.

But now the inauguration had happened. And it had *definitely* happened. A small crowd of humans had been there to verify it. (Zing.) There was no going back. And as we marched forward, the chants broke and scattered. We were approaching Trump Tower.

Trump Tower. What a dumb building. If you were going to create an evil-villain opposite of the White House, even the hackiest fantasy writer would reject the idea of a dark tower at this point (no offense, Stephen King—you got there early). But here it was, looming in front of us: a dark fucking jagged tower of black windows, which, even though it is fifty-eight stories, feels squat, brutish, feebly imagined. Why not put a glowing red eye on top, if you're going to be this on the nose?

This? I remember thinking. *This is what we fell for? Really? A literal dark tower? With a room of gold at the top and a gross monster smiling there amid his junky hoard of old newspapers and self-honoring awards, sneering over a taco bowl and dreaming of a magic wall?* It was ridiculous. And yet even in our outrage, we were still walking to the tower, drawn to it, gathering in its shadow.

It's not an ad hominem attack to call Trump a gross monster. You know what he looks like. His body makes no physical sense. You've seen the impossible hair and ties and tan so often that you've stopped seeing them, even though you can't look away. We don't control what we look like, but at the same time, these are choices Trump made. Maybe they are canny, purposeful choices, or uncanny, gut instincts that have proven useful over time. Along with his tweets and deflections, his attacks and shameless lies, the hair and ties and tan are deployed on purpose to overwhelm your senses, to paralyze your mind with questions that can never be answered, because Donald Trump, I'm fairly certain, doesn't know the answers himself. Because his one want is to overpower your brain and then consume you, like the writhing, unknowable creature at the end of an H. P. Lovecraft story, and making himself look and act like a gross monster allows him to do that.

And we all fell for it. Even those of us who didn't vote for him underestimated him. We all saw Donald Trump callously shape his campaign into a metaphoric cudgel that would cause actual pain and terror, and not one of us managed to stop it. We all thought we were so smart.

The march quieted as we reached Trump Tower. A protest was staged at its doors, but the energy seemed to have flown from the crowd, and it was cold in the tower's shadow. My son and I joined the others who were walking away. My heels hurt. We would all be walking in this exquisite tightness for four more years at least. As we left, I spied a man through the second-floor window of an electronics store. He was wearing a VR helmet and he had his hands out, listlessly pew-pewing his guns in another world. I didn't blame him. This one was pretty depressing.

And now we have to accept it. In the months that followed, we all frantically reminded one another on the internet to not normalize the Trump presidency. But this is a dishonor to reality. The fact is, the Trump presidency and all that led to it was already normal, if unseen. Otherwise it would not have happened.

However, even if we have to accept Trump, I'm not sure Trump can. Yes, he can overpower an entire centuries-old democracy through sheer shameless monstrosity, but that power is also a weakness. Consider how often he has been rewarded for simply, briefly acting like a normal human being for a day, and how often he has rejected that reward by becoming an unpredictable weirdo again. By many accounts, all Trump has *ever* wanted was acceptance: from television audiences, the business community, New York society, his dad. Seeking acceptance is what made him want this job in the first place, and now he's trapped in it. While writing this, I went back to look at that 2016 photo of Trump eating a taco bowl and loving "Hispanics," and I was struck by how happy—genuinely, even almost appealingly happy, even to me—he seemed back then, in his tower with his trash and trophies. Especially compared to how he seems now: a seething, addled minotaur at the center of a labyrinth he made and despises. We are trapped in there with him, and we are all trying to find our way out. We will.

I DON'T REMEMBER HOW MANY days after the election it was before my son and I started listening to music in the car again. He didn't play DJ Khaled anymore. We were tired of all the winning. Instead, he asked if I could search for "This Land Is Your Land" on my phone. I said, "Sure." He asked me if we could roll the windows down and play it loud as we drove home. We did, and I turned up the bass. I didn't tell him that we probably didn't have many minds to change outside the ramen shops and used bookstores on Vanderbilt Avenue in Prospect Heights, Brooklyn (but honestly, who knows?). I didn't tell him that a liberal dad and son blasting Woody Guthrie out of their eight-year-old VW Passat wagon was a little on the nose. But we live in unsubtle times. And in a couple of years, presuming there is still an America, we will all go back to the YMCA to vote again. My daughter will be with me again when I cast my vote, and then, this time, she will cast her own.

Chapter Eighteen

TWO BUILDINGS
IN FLORIDA

A s you have read, I have gotten into a lot of secret rooms, but there were two that I could not crack, and they were both in Florida.

I had gone to Florida to tour with the Boston Pops. I had performed comedy with the Pops a couple of years before. They had asked me to join their program as the narrator of Benjamin Britten's "The Young Person's Guide to the Orchestra." Instead of reading the traditional text describing the various instruments and sections of the orchestra, they asked me to write new, fake facts about those things. I was hesitant at first. It had been a while since I made up fake facts about musical instruments. I was trying to be more personal and honest and even transgressive in my comedy. I was self-conscious at the time that I was not a *real* comedian who pushed boundaries, made social statements, and discussed masturbation schedules.

But I had grown up going to Symphony Hall and could not resist the chance to perform on that stage. And it was thrilling.

I didn't make any masturbation jokes. I told the audience how the orchestra is organized into families, like *Game of Thrones*-land, but less peaceful. I told them about how the French horn players have the bell of their instruments attached to their hands at birth, and how the brass family is better than the reedy blow tubes that make up the woodwinds because they are made of real metal. You can melt trombones down and make them into swords when society collapses. This material killed. And I thought, *Oh, this is who I am. My comedy is not really speaking truth to power as it is making cello jokes at symphony subscribers, plus my dad and my mother-in-law.*

I built a very self-serving gag into the end of my script, where I told the audience that now the whole orchestra would play together, and I will eat a cheese sandwich. At this point the stage manager brought out a silver platter bearing an American cheese sandwich on the whitest bread, and I would eat it and listen to the Boston Pops right from the stage, the music blasting into my body and pushing my face into the biggest smile.

So when they asked, "Would you like to come on tour with us in Florida?" I replied with an automatic yes. I was still high on music and cheese. I didn't think at first about how going on tour in Florida in February was not the same as going to my hometown during the full spring bloom of May. I didn't think about how I would not be walking to Symphony Hall from the very nice hotel they put me up in, but driving at night on a bus from Fort Lauderdale to Sarasota to Orlando to Jacksonville and then down to Palm Beach with a bunch of musicians I did not know. I didn't know how long the distances between those places were, and what a strange crisscross route across the state they described, or how exhausted I would be.

But it's my policy to say yes, as you know, and that was how I ended up away from my family yet again, in a series of green rooms night after night, waiting like an instrument in a case until it was my time to go on. I would say my jokes about the oboes and double basses and eat my cheese sandwich. This took about twenty minutes. Then I would go back to my dressing room and look at Twitter for another hour, listening to the Pops cover "Pinball Wizard" over the speakers in my room. The audience was older, largely subscribers to the various performing arts centers we played who were just looking for a night out. More than once I heard a man say to his partner in the lobby before the show, "What are we seeing again?" I hope I didn't confuse them too much.

I didn't have to ride on the tour bus, though. Instead, I convinced my friend David Rees to come down and rent a car and split the driving with me. He had only one condition, which was that he wanted to see the Flag Land Base, one of the headquarters of the Church of Scientology. This condition was not going to be a problem for me. As a longtime, late-night, goggle-eyed fan of every Scientology training video on YouTube, I was only angry at myself for not thinking of it first. If you don't know, Scientology was founded by a writer named L. Ron Hubbard, who discarded his body on purpose in 1986, and it is now run by a man named David Miscavige. It is a major world religion just like any other major world religion, and that is all I am going to say, because I do not want David Miscavige to get mad at me again.

So after our show in Sarasota, David and I drove north across Tampa Bay to St. Petersburg and then into Clearwater. I don't remember what kind of car we rented, but David was driving.

As he drove, I told him what I had learned from the internet about the Flag Land Base. For years, L. Ron Hubbard ran Scientology from a fleet of three ships that constantly moved from port to port. He called himself the Commodore, and his elite clergy wore quasi-naval uniforms and were called the Sea Org (for "Sea Organization"). Eventually he wanted a land base, so Scientology purchased the Fort Harrison Hotel and named it Flag. It is where Scientologists go to receive the upper levels of Scientology training and scripture. But not the *highest* level. That's level OT VIII and it's only administered on the Scientology cruise ship called *Freewinds*. Different story.

"Wow," David Rees said. "You know a lot more about Scientology than I thought."

"Affirmative," I said.

Then, at 2000 hours, Friday, the 24th of January, 1986, L. Ron Hubbard discarded the body he had used in this lifetime for 74 years, 10 months, and 11 days. That's how David Miscavige described the death of L. Ron Hubbard. Then David Miscavige took charge of the church.

David Miscavige wanted to expand the Flag Land Base. For

years he raised funds from the membership to do this—some say more than it cost to build the building—and after a long period of on-again, off-again construction, the new Flag opened, connected to the old Flag by a sky bridge. It was the largest building in Clearwater. And while it is currently just called Flag, it was originally to be called the Super Power Building.

"WHAT?!" David Rees said in loud, joyous disbelief. "Super Powers?"

"It's true," I said. I explained that Scientology does not believe we have only five senses, but fifty-seven. According to the internet, these perceptics include: Time, Sight; Taste, Color, Depth; Touch (pressure, friction, heat or cold and oiliness); Personal emotion; Cellular and bacterial position; Saline content of self (body); Perception of having perceived (past and present); Awareness of not knowing; Awareness of importance, unimportance; Awareness of others; and hunger.

I told David that, supposedly, the new building includes training stations designed to help raise each perceptic to its highest ability. According to documents leaked to the internet that purport to be blueprints of the building, these stations include an antigravity machine, a time machine, a pain station, an infinite pit, and an oiliness table.

"Are you kidding me right now?" David Rees said. "We are definitely going inside *that* building! I am going to see that oiliness table."

"No, we're not," I said. "And no, you aren't."

The Flag Land Base is in downtown Clearwater, just before

the causeway that carries you to the beach. As we drove in on Court Street we could see it from far away: a giant, square, cream-frosted cake of a building with an eight-pointed Scientology star on top. When we first spotted it, we were driving through a charming, dumpy bustle of small motels, strip malls, chain restaurants, and a lot full of modded-out Jeeps called Jeff's Jeep Yard. But as we neared downtown, all that bustle dwindled to nothing. The office buildings were dull and blank. The sidewalks were gleaming and empty in the sun. We were the only car on the road.

We turned right and saw the sky bridge that connects the old building and the new. We passed under it and did a quick drive around the new building. The main entrance was a set of stairs between two pillars. The door was closed and no one seemed to be around. It was the bright middle of the day, and we did not see any humans anywhere. David finally pulled up to one of the dozens of empty parking meters and we idled on the arid, dead planet of Clearwater, Florida.

"This is weird," said David Rees. I agreed. It was weirder than I thought it would be. There was no question we were being surveilled, at least passively. I could see the glassy black domes hiding security cameras above doorways and under ledges. The church is famously secretive and paranoid of incursion. There are many videos online of people approaching the doors of various church buildings to protest or ask pointed questions of the church. Why they would want to protest a major world religion, I DO *NOT* KNOW. Often in these videos a member of the church will come out. They do not speak. They will just take out their own camera and start filming the person taking the video. It's unclear why they do this. But I know they keep track of their enemies. I was one of them.

I had made David Miscavige mad early in the 2000s by making a dumb joke about Scientology in *GQ* magazine. I say it was dumb because it used the classically lazy fifth-grade anus/ Uranus construction. I will tell you the joke someday if we run into each other. But I will not write it here, because I do not want what happened next to happen again. The joke was also dumb as in "unwise." Because after it was published, my editor said the Church of Scientology wanted to talk to me.

"No thank you," I said.

"That's fine," my editor said. "I'm here to protect you."

A week later he called again. "They *really* want to talk to you," he said.

"I really don't want to," I said.

"No problem," he said. "But I did give them your email."

"Why?" I asked.

"They were very persistent," he said. "And a little scary."

The next day I received a long email from a church publicist explaining that Scientology is a major world religion that is just like any other major world religion. *I wouldn't make a joke about Judaism, would I?* the church publicist asked. (FYI, Judaism is also a major world religion just like Scientology, with the small difference that it has been around for five thousand years, and they don't charge you money to read the Torah.) Anyway, the point was, I was a terrible bigot. But I was also a lucky bigot, because a little Scientology could help me with that problem.

I ignored the email, and then I received another one. I don't recall if I got a third. Those emails are on a dead computer in a basement in Massachusetts now. I do remember that the name of the publicist was Karin Pouw, who is a real person. But I've since read theories on the internet that David Miscavige himself often writes angry letters under her name. I hope so. I like to roll with the bigs.

Whoever it was, they were persistent and they were also scary. The content of the letters didn't concern me. Honestly, my joke was terrible, and I deserved the punishment. What unnerved me was the follow-through. This was around 2001. *GQ* did not have a website then. There were no Google alerts popping up at Flag Land Base to let the church know that John Hodgman had made a dumb joke. And what's more, my name wasn't even bylined on the piece. This meant that in 2001, some Sea Org member was tasked to read every page of *GQ* every month, in some basement room full of other Sea Org members reading every other magazine and newspaper, just looking for even the smallest mentions of Scientology. Even the dumbest, unbylined little front-of-the-book squib would then be passed up the chain of command, a call would be made, an email address would be obtained, and letters would be written. Just to let me know: *they were watching*.

For all I knew, they were still watching. For all I knew, there was still a basement room full of Sea Org members here in

Clearwater who all knew my name. As an egotist, this was exciting, but I did not want to provoke them to action.

"You're being paranoid," David said. "Let's at least *try* to get in there."

"I don't even want to get out of the car anymore," I said.

"Let's just walk around the building once," David said. "Check the perimeter."

"Fine," I said. I got out and put some quarters in the parking meter, but it was out of order.

At the northwest corner of the Super Power Building, we found a wall of windows beneath swirling letters that read "FLAG." We couldn't see through the wall of windows. They were all tinted black, as were the glass doors that now opened quickly and then shut. A woman had come out. She was skinny and pale, wearing dark glasses and a headscarf that reminded me of the scarves people sometimes cover their scalps with when undergoing chemotherapy. She walked by us without speaking, as if we were not there.

We walked on along the north and east faces of the building, admiring more opaque windows and surveillance cameras. There was a loading bay. "Maybe we can get in there," said David. But the door did not open. The building felt abandoned.

Then we turned right again into the bright sunlight and utter silence of the east face, across from a half-full parking lot of lifeless cars. We had stopped talking by then. We wanted to get this over with.

We turned the corner into the full Florida heat and glare

that poured onto the southern face. This was where the main entrance was. When we had driven around once before, there had been no one there, of course. But now there were four people there: two men and two women, all in black slacks and white shirts and vests with golden trim. They were members of the Sea Org, all waiting at attention, all staring into the sun.

They were not waiting there for us. They were waiting to greet a shuttle bus of Scientologists, but it hadn't arrived yet. I don't remember how we learned that, or when. The Sea Org didn't tell us. They just stared straight ahead as we passed them. Maybe some secret sense of shuttle-bus awareness had been awakened in me by some machine within the Super Power Building. Certainly all of my *known* perceptics were firing hard as we walked past their blank faces. We were all of us alive with an electric awareness of perceiving and being perceived. The strangeness of it all hit my body in a queasy, physical wave.

We didn't stop walking. David said, "Hi, sorry," as we passed, and one Sea Org member, a man, not quite turning his head, gave a slightly sheepish "Hey there" back. At that moment, another Sea Org member, a woman, not quite turning her head, murdered the first man with her eyes.

They weren't there for us, but they knew what we were up to. How many of us gawkers had come walking by before, trying to get a look at their infinite pit? I felt bad for them now, having to pretend not to see us. But on the other hand, we justified their paranoia. That had to make them feel good. What if no one *ever* came to gawk?

We reached the far corner and our hearts were pounding and our oiliness was off the charts. "That was the weirdest thing I have ever experienced," David said, and I agreed that was true, until we turned the next and final corner. That's when we saw a man taking a photo of our car and license plate.

It freaked us out, but I confess I felt a little vindicated. They really were surveilling us after all! Now *my* paranoia had been justified. The mysterious man moved on to take pictures of other parked cars, and we were glad to get in our rental and get out of there. As I say, I don't remember what kind of car it was. So if you're a Sea Org member charged with reading this as part of your intelligence gathering on me, please look in my file for the photo the mysterious man took and let me know the make and model. It would be a nice detail to include in the paperback.

Clearwater had been a detour, so David and I had a hard, fast drive across central Florida to rejoin the Pops in Orlando. I realize now that I sounded pretty down on the tour earlier, but it ended up being a lot of fun. The musicians were all incredibly nice. As they were older, a lot of them remembered that I had been on television once, which was nice, but others revealed even deeper connections. One violinist was the daughter of Mr. Wright, who taught me Russian history in high school. A violist named Scott told me that one of his students had bought the viola that I used to own and play on. (Yeah, I talk about the clarinet a lot, but I also played viola. That's right: I crossed the strings/woodwinds streams. Deal with it.) Scott showed me a photo of his student holding my old viola. They were both strangers to me, but I was touched to see these extended members of my family. We were all weird thirteen-year-olds who had grown up. Many of these musicians didn't even play with the Pops regularly. They were the touring company, orchestra carnies sleeping on a bus, putting a living together just to keep doing what they loved. I was proud to be with them.

Each night I would eat my cheese sandwich and get my polite chuckles. Then the Pops would do, say, an orchestral version of "Stairway to Heaven" and the crowd would be on its feet in rapturous applause. At first I felt insecure about being upstaged night after night by orchestral oldies, but people like what they like. And honestly, if you're only hearing the Pops through the PA in your green room, you don't get the full, loud, joyously goofy effect of having "All About That Bass" plowed right into your midsection on a live sousaphone. At the last concert David Rees and I took edibles and went out into the house for their cover of "Bohemian Rhapsody" and yes, we sang along, and yes, we banged our heads, just like everyone else.

After the shows, most of the orchestra would go to bed, but there was always a clutch of violinists we could join at the hotel bar, and let me tell you: the violin section goes *hard*. They stay up late and talk in fake accents, they get deep and confessional, and then when you are going to bed, they go off to smoke marijuana out of a trumpet mouthpiece with some of the guys in the brass section. I told you that the brass instruments were practical.

And if I sounded sour on Florida, I apologize and take that back too, because I had a really nice time in Florida. There is a cliché about Florida on the internet that it is all one eccentric, violent, dumb place, home to eccentric, violent, dumb Florida Men who are constantly fistfighting raccoons and wandering drunk into Costcos wearing only a gimme hat, a loincloth made of pancakes, and a machete. While this Florida may exist, there are of course dozens of Floridas, all of them beautiful, impossible landscapes. I took a water bus through the canals that snake among the glass towers of Fort Lauderdale and felt like I was on the cover of a paperback science fiction novel. And then we drove west through the ancient hot mess of the Everglades and Big Cypress National Preserve, empty except for cows swamp-grazing by the side of the road. We nosed our car past the darkened, empty hotels of Daytona Beach, too early for the season, and in St. Augustine I found a vintage Griswold cast-iron pan that had been enameled: white on the inside, fire engine red on the outside. I have never seen anything like it before.

Florida is upside-down land in that the farther north you drive, the closer you get, physically and culturally, to the conservative, evangelical American South. Jacksonville is Trump territory, and we found it grim and sterile at first. But I *can* recommend the Ibex Ethiopian Kitchen on Baymeadows Road. The owner is an incredibly nice man who will sit with you and keep you company as you eat your *alicha wot* and chicken *sambusa*s, because at 3 p.m., you will be the only customers there.

Try to go on a February 4th, if you can, because maybe the owner's daughter will come back and have another birthday party there. She was turning thirteen when we were there, and as we were finishing our food, she and a bunch of her friends and their parents filled the place with balloons and cake and pizzas. They were all Ethiopian or Ethiopian American. We started to leave, but her dad said, "Please stay," so we did. We watched as they played various party games and then broke for food: the parents ate Ethiopian food and the daughter and her teen friends ate pizza and talked about the election. "I mean, who the hell *is* Gary Johnson, anyway?" one boy said, and the teenagers broke into laughing agreement. It was a nice reminder in the heart of Trump country that America is already great and getting greater.

The Pops had the next night off and were all going to stay behind in Jacksonville. But David and I pushed on toward Palm Beach. As we drove, we realized two things: First, it was Super Bowl Sunday. And second: we were going to Palm Beach. *That* Palm Beach. It had been a short enough time since the election that, even when we saw the itinerary, the location of Mar-a-Lago was still vague to us, a different, tawdry dimension that we would never visit. But now we were on our way there, and so was Donald Trump.

"I totally want to get in there," David said.

"No thank you," I said.

"I bet we could," David said. "I feel like anyone could walk in there if they looked enough like a ridiculous billionaire or a servant."

"Maybe," I said.

"If you *could* get in," David said, "if you could get close to him, would you try to take him out?"

Attention, Scientology Sea Org member assigned to read this book in a basement somewhere: Obviously my friend David Rees was not actually plotting to murder Donald Trump. It is important to remember that we were still in shock at this time. We were in a twisting, unrecognizable forest of emotions, and we were trying to find our way back to any recognizable landscape, and sometimes our wanderings took dark paths.

In any case, I told David no. Absolutely not. Murder is wrong, first of all. And Donald Trump getting attacked by a person from New England who used to work on *The Daily Show* and is now touring with the Boston Pops would only make Donald Trump a hero and confirm the paranoia of his followers.

"Maybe you're right," said David. "Let me ask you this," he continued. "If you could slip into his room and secretly give him a drug and slip out, would you do that?"

"What drug?" I asked.

"It would make him two feet tall overnight. It would be irreversible, and no one would know what caused it."

I thought about it. We both did. We tried to imagine the ramifications of this. We tried to imagine how the *New York Times* would handle the push notification of this news: "President Trump is now two feet tall, baffling experts."

Finally, I sighed. "Let's not talk about the impossible."

We were back on Route A1A, and as I looked at the map, we

saw its path went straight through West Palm Beach, over the causeway to Palm Beach proper. Then it hit the beach at South Ocean Boulevard and turned right, directly past Mar-a-Lago. Our path seemed fated, so we agreed to at least drive by it. But when we reached the right turn that led to the winter White House, all we saw were flashing blue lights. Twin sheriff cars were blocking the road, and they turned us away. Trump had already arrived.

David was frustrated as we made our way back along South Ocean Boulevard, the beach to our right, mansions shielded by tall topiary walls to our left. I was too. A public road had been closed to us so that a rich man could watch the Super Bowl in his playhouse and show his rich friends the nuclear football. But I was relieved to leave Mar-a-Lago behind us.

We went back into West Palm Beach, checked into our hotel, and went out in search of dinner. We walked past the imposing Palm Beach County Courthouse, glass towers atop a giant pale stone archway flanked by tall palms, all lit in pink searchlights—an aesthetic David described as "coral fascist." We turned onto Clematis Street and found a restaurant with a tin ceiling and little marble tables offering craft cocktails and pork belly. You spend enough time on the road and you realize that there are little Brooklyns everywhere.

The food was good, and we felt at home. The manager, Andrew, said, "It's John Hodgman!" and also "It's David Rees!" which made us both feel very good about how the evening was going to go. He introduced us to two of his friends, Josh and

Christa, who were getting married. They were all in their thirties and starting their adulthoods and it was fun to talk to them and steal their life essence. Though it was a Brooklyn-style restaurant, there was still a television in the corner, and the Super Bowl was on it. But even this enhanced the evening, because the Falcons were playing the New England Patriots, and the New England Patriots were going to lose. David Rees promised me this.

David Rees knows more about sports than I do, so I had no reason to distrust him as the game progressed and he grew happier. I grew happy as well. I do not know the rules to football but this was one time where I at least understood the narrative. Trump was a Patriots fan, and Tom Brady and Bob Kraft were friends of Trump. The Pats were a dynasty, constant glib, grinning winners who never *really* got punished, even when they were cheating. The Falcons were an underdog, who were now, cathartically, going to beat the Patriots, *finally*. Every time the Falcons put the ball in the score hole or whatever, David cheered and the bar cheered and even I cheered, because even though I didn't know what had happened, I knew that Donald Trump was just a little ways away in his tacky palace, also watching the game, feeling sad.

The Falcons went on winning, and we did not get tired of it. Soon we learned that Donald Trump had left his own party and gone to bed. He knew he was beaten. It reminded me of my own retreat to bed when the election results came in. I was joyous. I have never enjoyed football more in my life. More drinks, more cheers, and David ordered frogs legs. I posted a photo of him eating them, grinning, offering a gloating thumbs-up to all the alt-right creeps with their "Pepe the Frog" avatars out there who had previously laughed at our pain and drunk our liberal tears. Victory was ours.

"This is amazing," David said. "No one has ever had a lead like this in football. It is statistically impossible for the Patriots to win at this point."

This is when I stopped feeling good. "David," I said. "Is this starting to feel a little like Election Night to you?"

David's eyes narrowed a bit. He wordlessly got up and walked to the far end of the bar to watch the game alone. I don't think he was mad at me. I think he simply recoiled from me and my awful words before they could ensnare his imagination and strangle it in dread. I think he wanted to survive.

Of course the Patriots did win. I followed their progress on my phone, alone at the table, occasionally looking to David, standing by himself, staring up into the television. The Patriots impossibly plodded back to victory and shoved it right in my friend's face. I was so mad. It was not enough to have to go through it again, the whiplash change of fortune, the nauseating swivel from relief and hope to confusion and despair. But on top of everything, Trump had tricked me into caring about the Super Bowl.

But David took it even harder. His eyes were dark and haunted. "Andrew," he said. "Is there a place in town you can recommend where we can go punch some Patriots fans?"

Andrew pointed us sympathetically to some second location. We went, but we didn't punch anybody. And I don't remember what happened after that other than that I spent all
my money and woke up in the morning with a picture on my
phone I didn't remember taking, of a photograph of Tom Waits
hanging in a restaurant bathroom somewhere in West Palm
Beach, Florida.

The next day David and I met for coffee. We had a whole day
before I was to perform that night. We decided to go to the actual beach on Palm Beach. We drove over there, found parking
easily, and set up in the shade of the retaining wall at the top of
the beach. One difference between Florida and Maine, of course,
is that the beaches in Florida are soft and comforting, and that
was what we needed. We swam in the warm ocean and watched
airplanes fly away. We wondered if any of them were Air Force
One. We felt better.

After a while, David went to go check out the Palm Beach
Goodwill, I stayed behind and read a book. Though Palm
Beach itself feels like a cross between a gated community, a
luxury mall, and one giant outdoor Mercedes-Benz dealership,
the beach itself was public and chill. It was the middle of a
Monday, and there were the standard, marginal beach people
there, students and moms with kids and skinny dudes with
devil sticks. One incredibly handsome young black couple set
two chairs up about fifteen feet away from me and relaxed with
placid determination. It felt like they were giving no ground.

One thing you should do if you are in Palm Beach is go to

the Goodwill. I regret that I didn't. David sent me photos of rack after rack of barely worn Brooks Brothers suits and dress shirts . . . the discarded wardrobes of countless dead rich husbands. But David only purchased a short-sleeved navy button-down and white linen shorts.

"Do I look like a pool boy?" he asked.

"I guess so," I said.

"Good. I want to go over to Mar-a-Lago and tell them I'm the new pool boy."

I didn't want to do this. Unlike sneaking into the Flag Land Base, which was always halfway a joke, I could tell he meant it this time. I even thought he might be able to do it, as he was possessed now by new, sad, mad purpose. But I also knew that as his friend, I at least had to go with him to the gates and give him a chance to shed that purpose before it consumed him.

We drove back along South Ocean Boulevard, the beach on our left this time, reversing our retreat of the night before.

"I'm David, I work at the pool," David rehearsed as he drove. "I'm new here," he said. "I'm David. I work at the pool."

As we approached the intersection of where we had been turned away, I saw that the sheriff's cars were gone. Instead there was an illuminated police sign that flashed a warning: "TRAVELING CRIMINALS IN AREA." *That is us*, I thought as we passed it. *We are the traveling criminals.* I was so scared.

But there was no one around Mar-a-Lago. It was not even clear where we were supposed to drive in. As soon as we saw it, we had passed it. At the next intersection, we pulled a U-turn and backtracked, this time more slowly. There it was. What a dumb house.

Mar-a-Lago was built between 1924 and 1927 by Marjorie Merriweather Post, a socialite who inherited her father's cereal company and eventually became the richest woman in America. Its outside is dumb, gaudy, pink, and covered in bad mosaics. I have never seen any of its fifty-eight bedrooms or thirty-three bathrooms or three bomb shelters, but I bet they are dumb too. She built it as a place to live with her husband, who apparently could not use the same bathroom twice in one month. It is called Mar-a-Lago to indicate that its property stretches from the ocean to the lake, but this is also dumb, because the lake to the west isn't a lake, but Florida's Intracoastal Waterway. The ocean to the east is definitely an ocean, but critically, Mar-a-Lago's property doesn't quite stretch beyond the road where we idled now, so the house isn't only dumb, it's also a liar.

When she died in 1972, Marjorie Merriweather Post willed the mansion to the National Park Service, offering its use as a winter White House for the president, and that is absolutely true. But none of the presidents wanted it, and it was expensive to maintain, so the government said no thank you and gave it back to the estate in 1981.

It was then listed for sale for $20 million, but no one else wanted it either, because it's dumb. That's when Donald Trump heard about it. He *definitely* wanted that dumb house, and he offered $15 million, which the Post Foundation should have taken. But they rejected him because they thought Donald

Trump was worse than they were. They were snobs, but they were right.

Because their property did not stretch to the ocean, there was a strip of land between South Ocean Boulevard and the beach, and Donald Trump bought it for $2 million. He threatened to build a home there specifically to block Mar-a-Lago's view. The Post Foundation said, please don't do that, you can have the house for $15 million. But now Donald Trump said "nope" and forced it out of them for less than $8 million in 1985. I don't know whether *that* was when he learned that assholism works, or if he learned it before then. Wikipedia doesn't say anything about that.

As we sized up Mar-a-Lago, we watched a man on a ten-speed bike slowly pedal by it in the opposite lane. The moment he hit the property line, he raised his middle finger to the house and kept it that way until he reached the opposite property line. It felt like he did that every day.

"Let's pull in there," said David. He pointed to a small, short driveway leading up to a white gate that was tall, narrow, and closed. We nosed our car right up to the gate. It was a side entrance, but it was still baubled with twinkly junk: twin statues of sailors and ceramic tiles bearing the same motto I had seen on the wall behind Donald Trump when he posted the photo of him fake-writing his inaugural address: *Plus Ultra.* Beyond the ultimate.

The gate was closed. It was made of thick white bars studded with decorative spheres. You could see right through it. You could touch it, but I didn't want to. Like Flag, it felt electric to stand there, the place where the sick, artless dreams of not one but *two* rich clods had come true. *This is where it comes from*, I remember thinking. *All this pain*. But I did touch the gate. It was cathartic. And we realized: the gate is made of wood.

"I want to get in there," David said.

"No," I said. But not because it was so closely guarded. In fact, there was no one there at all. I saw no surveillance cameras. No guards. No one taking pictures of us or our car.

"I don't think anyone's home," I said.

We stayed in that narrow driveway for a long time. We took pictures through the gate. I took pictures of David wearing his pool boy uniform. No one ever came for us. We didn't get in, but we felt a little better. We learned that day that the Church of Scientology has better security than the winter White House. As I write this, I have learned that a Chinese woman recently talked her way in with a purse full of suspicious tech and thumb-drives stuffed with malware—maybe even a magical shrink-you-to-two-foot-high pill—so I don't think they've upped their game since we were there. But we are not traveling criminals. We went home.

Oh, I just realized I have that photo of David in his phony uniform at the gate, and it shows our car in it. So stand down, Church of Scientology. It was a white Toyota Avalon.

Chapter Nineteen

A MAN GOES ON
A JOURNEY

I t was 3 a.m. now in my kitchen, the light barely chasing away the deep night dark in the corners. The flight had been chosen. My passenger information and credit card security code had been entered. My finger hovered over the trackpad, guiding the pointer that hovered over the "Confirm and Buy" button. I waited. I made my decision.

Did you think I bought that expensive plane ticket just to become Diamond? No. I took a deep breath and closed the window.

But then, a day or two later, a miracle happened. A public radio program in Portland, Oregon, called *Live Wire Radio* contacted me. They said that Bruce Campbell had canceled their December taping. His mother had fallen and hurt herself. As a friend of *Live Wire*, and a friend of public radio, and a friend of Bruce Campbell, and a friend of all mothers everywhere, would I consider doing the show? It was going to happen this weekend, but it would be easy. All I would need to do is be interviewed onstage for fifteen minutes.

I said, "No thank you." I wrote an email to say I was taking a break from travel for the sake of my family and my own exhausted body. But then I deleted that email. I checked my Beloved Airlines web page and mapped out a flight. I wrote to them and said yes, so long as they booked me on *this* specific flight.

"OK," they said.

I told them it would have to be first class. Otherwise I wouldn't get the MQMs I needed. I presumed this was not in their budget. But I knew *they* were desperate, and what I was doing was terrible. I was holding a public radio show hostage so that I could fly there Platinum and come back Diamond. But I said nothing and waited for their answer.

"OK," they said.

Before I flew out, Luke Burbank, the host, called me to ask what I wanted to talk about. I realized I had no new jokes or stories to tell. I had no television projects to promote. I had nothing at all.

"I guess I'd like to talk about my frequent flyer program," I said.

"Oh thank God," said Luke. "Me too. It's all I think about." Because he is also a middle-aged man who must use consumer benchmarks to convince himself he is still desirable.

That Friday night I flew overnight on Beloved Airlines to Portland. I was in first class. I asked for a whiskey from the flight attendant, and she poured me a double that put me right to sleep. Two hours later I woke up briefly from a dream. I noticed the glass was still in my hand, and the flight attendant had refilled it. While I was sleeping. Something was happening, I could tell. Beloved Airlines was beloving me. Unwisely, I drank the sleep whiskey and fell asleep again.

I was in Portland for less than twenty-four hours. The show went well. Luke and I had a grand old chat about our status addiction. I told the story about the Beloved One lounge. I told the story about how I nearly broke my son's heart to make Diamond, and how Luke's radio show finally allowed that to happen. Luke is not part of the Beloved Airlines ecosystem. He's an Alaska Airlines person. I know nothing about their program or their status levels, and I refuse to look it up. Halfway through our conversation, I realized that Alaska was also a sponsor of the show. I was sure they were not going to be pleased at all by all my buzz marketing for Beloved. Maybe they would pull their sponsorship. Maybe I was going to accidentally destroy this public radio show. I didn't mind. I would be on my way home by then.

Very early the next morning, I went to the airport. I don't remember if anyone was playing the piano in the Portland airport that morning. When I boarded the flight, two things suggested it was going to be a special flight. First, as I settled into my seat, a young man heading back to coach leaned over and whispered to me, "I am a member of Book and Snake," and then walked on. That's a true story.

Second, I realized that the flight crew was the same group I had flown with on my way to Portland. There was the same flight attendant, smiling at me. "Are you ready for your whiskey?" she asked. It was 7:30 in the morning. I knew she was not joking.

I realized that it was already happening. I was entering a new world of privilege where even the worst, most self-destructive behavior was not only tolerated, but encouraged. Because nothing could make me ugly anymore. I was becoming the most beautiful, brilliant, and hardest naturally occurring substance on earth.

On December 6, Beloved flight 1504 from Portland passed over the geometric center of the United States and I earned my 125,000th Medallion Qualifying Mile. And at precisely 2:36 p.m. Beloved Airlines Mean Time, John Hodgman went Diamond.

At that moment, there was a small ceremony. All the other passengers on the plane fell asleep. The flight attendants each came over and kissed me on the brow. Then they opened the secret eyeballs in the middle of their foreheads.

And they spoke to me in a screech language. It sounded like when they talk through the weird princess phones they keep by their little jump seats, but in this case, I could actually understand what they were saying.

"Thank you," they said. "Thank you for being Diamond."

They said even though this flight offered no lunch service, they had a secret lunch they could offer me. A choice of microwaved short ribs or a squash lasagna. They were out of the chicken.

I noticed the plane had stopped moving. *How is this possible?* I wondered silently.

In my head, they responded: *It is not possible. Airflight is both unnatural and impossible. Just as you have always suspected. These planes are powered by mystic energy, channeling power emitted by pyramids in the Nile River delta. That is where we get our name.*

For of course, Beloved Airlines is Delta Airlines. There are no secrets among us anymore.

Something dripped into my eyes, and I realized that where the flight attendants had kissed me on my forehead, I had opened my own third eye, forming the triangle of a delta, and my delta eye was crying.

They told me not to cry, not with any of my eyes. Now that I am Diamond, I would be free from sadness, free from pain.

They said I can literally not be cut or wounded. So better not to schedule any surgery.

Because now I had value. Now a major corporation loves me, and would continue to love me forever.

Just kidding. Only for one year.

Chapter Twenty

A STRANGER COMES
TO TOWN

O K. I was lying at the start of this book. I do have one
more story from Maine to tell you. I wasn't sure about
including it, for reasons that may be obvious. But I felt I had to,
so I'm just hiding it here at the end of the book, a place very few
people will travel to.

The general store in our town in Maine has a new kitchen
that was put in by new owners, and they are very generous. They
sell breakfast sandwiches there, and they let me help make
them on Sundays, if I feel like it. I *always* feel like it. Eggs start
as disgusting snotty chaos. Every time you crack one into a pan,
it's already a disaster, but it's a disaster that you can learn to
coax into pleasing order—not *all* the time, but at a higher rate
than life normally offers. And melting cheese is always a worth-
while thing to do. You know this.

I can disappear into making breakfast sandwiches, and as I
get older, I often feel that is a good final outcome for me. A
couple of years ago, the Store had come up for sale. I spent

some real time considering giving up all my other jobs, plus all my money, and buying it. But this idea was vetoed. While both my wife and son would happily move to Maine full-time tomorrow, that is our teenage daughter's literal nightmare.

"I had the dream again where I come home from school and you say we are moving to Maine," she has told us more than once. "And then in the dream I kill you both in your sleep."

She does not actually say the last part, but her eyes do.

I am lucky for her input, for it turned out, I was not quite ready to give up all my other jobs, as evidenced by all those stories I told you earlier in this book. And also, it was soon discovered that the Store, which had stood at the intersection of the one road and the other road in town since 1872, should not be standing at all. It had no foundation or a basement or proper drainage. An inspection revealed that the wood beams that had once formed the walls had gradually been replaced by rot and rat feces, more or less. So I am grateful to the new owners for buying it instead of me. I am grateful they tore the old store down by touching its structure once gently with a backhoe and then letting a baby breathe on it. And I'm grateful for their building a new Store that essentially saved the town and for giving me a nice place to make eggs in.

I love warming up the big square stainless-steel griddle. I love scraping it clean. I love timing out the muffin toasting, and the bacon drop. The store uses cheddar, but I bring in my own white American cheese, because I like my cheese the way I like my privilege. And yes, we use mayonnaise, at least whenever

I'm working. Go scream in someone else's comments about this. We use a squeeze bottle, and every sandwich literally bears the mayonnaise initial *J* inside. Because I stand by my principles: it tastes good, and it will not change.

I love wrapping the sandwiches in little squares of foil-lined paper and bundling them into the warmer out front so the sandwiches can steep, properly, for hours. I do *not* love it when a customer catches me out there and yells at me. They yell because we ran out of sausage sandwiches too fast. Or else they yell because they want a special sandwich, no sausage, for example, or no mayo. It's usually the wealthy summer people (like me) who yell for special treatment because they suspect that in life they are unspecial, and they are correct, and this knowledge hurts them. When they yell at me, they do not know that I am not a paid employee. They don't know it's just my hobby, so I suck it up and suffer the yelling. It reminds me that most service workers are not doing it as performance art, and often they are humiliated by customers like this every day, not just on Sundays.

I was trained in the kitchen by Tom, and when I go in on Sundays we work the griddle side by side. Tom is not an employee either: just another breakfast sandwich dilettante. Tom is a little older than I am. He is in insurance of some fashion, and on Sundays he comes in to the Store to work and tell dad jokes. He has a sailboat in the harbor, and painted on its side in too-big letters is its name: *After You.* If you tell Tom you like his boat, he says, "Thank you. I named it *after you.*" I have heard him say this so many times.

A couple of years ago, New Year's Eve fell on a Sunday. I wasn't working that day, but we were in town, and we went to the Store in the afternoon to see who was hanging around. The Store was busy. The temperature had not risen above 10 degrees for five days, and that was at noon. The bay had frozen over. People were restless and wanted to see other humans and feel normal.

My daughter was already at the Store, working the register alongside her friend, another teenager named Fiona. My daughter does not want to live in Maine, but she likes to work at the Store when she is in town. She does this because she is responsible and independent. I also presume she wants to absorb the experience of small-town life so she can make money off it when she goes back to the city, just like her dad. Fiona, on the other hand, is a local and a native, with generations of family history on this peninsula. Fiona works at the Store because she does everything.

I was not cooking eggs that morning, but Tom was. When I arrived, he took me aside.

"Do you want a pancake?" he said in a whisper.

"Tom," I said. "What are you talking about? We don't make pancakes. We make *breakfast sandwiches.*"

"We make pancakes now," Tom said. "Also: he's here."

Tom turned his head and I followed his eyes to a man sitting at a nearby table. This man was eating a pancake. He was the man who had bought the house in town that was once owned by a Famous Author. You remember the Famous Author's house from my last book. If you haven't figured out who that Famous Author is by now, here is a hint: It was not Leo Tolstoy. He lived in Russia. But Tolstoy did say that all of literature is either one of two stories, and here, sitting before me, was the second one: A stranger comes to town.

Very few people in town had actually seen the Stranger. He had come to buy the Famous Author's house at the beginning of the fall. Then he went back to his year-round home. Pennsylvania, I had heard. I had heard he was politically conservative and maybe a follower of Ayn Rand. I presumed he must be wealthy. The previous owners of the Famous Author's house, having more or less kept its literary pedigree quiet for thirty years, suddenly abandoned their discretion when it came time to sell. They gave a huge interview to a regional magazine about the legacy of the Famous Author's house and how they had been the caretakers of it, and then they asked a fortune for it, and the Stranger paid that fortune.

When we had arrived in town on Christmas Eve, we heard that the Stranger had come back from wherever else he lived and was starting to pop up around town. Some nights ago, we heard, he had materialized at the Pub, which is the half-finished basement beneath the Inn where people go to drink in winter. The Stranger asked the bartender, Shannon (who is Fiona's sister, if you wish to know), what there was to do in town (answer: go to the Pub) and whether there was a movie theater nearby (answer: nope). And then he transformed into a cloud of wasps and flew up the chimney!

That is not true, but it felt that way. He was a rumor around town, a shade, a Stephen King cliché. The mysterious new owner of old Famous Author Mansion. What was he up to in there? What were those strange lights in the window? What was that pungent smell? Was he holding rituals? Was he trying to conjure the ghost of Ayn Rand? That would have been very exciting for me, though frustrating for Ayn Rand, who did not believe in an afterlife.

It turns out the light and smoke were actually from a small kitchen fire. When he arrived, the Stranger had accidentally burned some scallops. Tom had told me about this, because Tom is also the deputy chief of the volunteer fire department, and he had responded to the call.

"We talked for a while," Tom had said. "He's an interesting guy."

But now, on New Year's Eve, the Stranger had revealed himself to all of us, in plain sight at the Store. He was dressed in a new plaid flannel shirt and a warm vest with many pockets. He was eating a blueberry pancake at a table with a few people, including Brian, who helps run the boatyard. You remember Brian? The one who told me the story from the last book about Jimmy Steele swearing at him? Brian is Fiona's dad, in case you were worried that this town was not small enough.

The Stranger was asking Brian what there was to do in town on New Year's Eve. Specifically, was anyone going to the First Night festival over in the neighboring, bigger town? Brian said probably not.

As they talked, the store grew busier. There was an aimless, nervous bustle among the people coming in. I had the impression that the word had spread: *The Stranger is here.* People drifted by his table, casting tentative glances at him. I confess I was a little angry about this. *I* was supposed to be the famous one in this town.

But small towns require neighborliness, so I sat down and told him my name. The Stranger didn't recognize it. Perhaps to spare my feelings, Tom produced a copy of *Vacationland*, my previous book, which is available in paperback in case you want to buy it. Tom asked me to sign it for a friend.

This alerted the Stranger's eyes, and he smiled. He asked me what kind of stuff I wrote. For a long moment, I didn't know what to say.

"Comedy, I guess," I said. But I could have gone on. I used to write and perform comedy. I used to be on television, and for a while I could not walk through an airport without people stopping me. But now that doesn't happen. Now I write halfway-funny true stories from my life and my own reflections on certain houses certain Strangers may have bought. But mostly, I make egg sandwiches.

The Stranger asked me what I was doing for New Year's Eve. I told him we were skipping First Night, but that afternoon we were going over to a nearby farm. My family had been offered a sleigh ride by a man named Curtis who has two Belgian draft horses named Mike and Skid.

The Stranger said that sounded great. Just the thing for

his kids, who were visiting. He said he was going to do the same thing.

"I . . . I'm not sure you can," I said. "I mean, I don't know. We just met Curtis last week. We bought a Christmas tree off him, and he was nice and offered us a sleigh ride. It was all sort of . . . informal."

The Stranger laughed me off. He asked me for Curtis's number, and I gave it to him. I wasn't sure if I should. But I did.

Then the Stranger got up and walked over to the refrigerator case full of nonorganic milk and bright-red hot dogs. He called Curtis up and organized a sleigh ride for himself, right after mine. Then he walked into the General Store kitchen. He didn't ask anyone if that was OK, and no one stopped him. He asked Tom to make some more pancakes, and Tom did.

I didn't understand what I was seeing. This was not the Maine of my experience. Just the day before, my daughter and I had driven to Stonington. Stonington lands more lobster than anywhere else in the world, but it got its name for the granite they used to quarry from the island across the harbor. That island is named Crotch Island, because there are a very large number of islands off the coast of Maine, and so I guess every other word in the world was taken.

In the summer, Stonington is full of tourists wandering happily in and out of the little galleries and shops that inhabit what were once the homes of the many Crotch Island commuters. But in the winter, everything is closed but the Harbor Cafe, which makes and serves the best tuna melt I have ever had in my life.

It was a little early for lunch, so the place was empty when my daughter and I walked in. We sat down at a large booth.

The woman server confronted us with immediate frustration. "This booth is for four people only. You can sit over *there*." We did, following her pointed finger to a smaller booth. We were not surprised by her gruffness. And we were not surprised when a man walked in—clearly a local and a regular—and was shown warmly to the four top we had just been banished from. We were not surprised that he sat there alone for an hour, eating a slice of chocolate cream pie as the restaurant got busier and busier. We were not surprised, and we were not offended. We had been in Maine long enough to know that her four-top rule was a lie. Or, I should say, to know that there were different rules for him and for us. And that was fine: as a local, he had earned that consideration.

We had only lived in our own town for a few summers. But things had gotten easier and friendlier since we first arrived. The postmaster, who had been consistently brusque with us since the day we met her, suddenly sweetened for no reason one July morning and went so far as to ask us how we were. It had only taken four years. And then one day, the grandson of the Famous Author, the owner of the boatyard whom I described at the end of my last book, called me by name. I do not know how or when he learned it. He didn't say, "It's John Hodgman!" He just said, "Hi, John," quietly, even blandly, one afternoon at the boatyard. It was the greatest thing to ever happen to me. Better than being Gold.

Back at the Harbor Cafe in Stonington, my daughter and I knew we might eventually get that big table and that slice of pie, but only after long years of following the orders given to us, until it was clear we knew why he is *there* and we are *here*. Maine is clarifying, because unlike on my Beloved Airlines, there is no round-trip ticket to Los Angeles you can buy to elevate your status. Admittance to Maine Medallion Status is awarded only for patience, a proof that you are sticking around, a proof that you respect and appreciate those who already have.

In this Maine, the Maine I *thought* I understood, if you cold-called a man named Curtis and demand he take you on a sleigh ride, you would be cursed at. I still trust that if the Stranger had wandered into the kitchen at the Harbor Cafe and asked for more pancakes, he would never have come out. But here at the Store in our town, the Stranger seemed to have us under a spell. I've met a number of people with wealth and power who feel rules don't apply to them. But this was different: a confident, not unpleasant, but relentless cheerfulness, that turned us into his thralls.

Later I would learn that when the Stranger came in, he asked Tom if they made pancakes.

Tom said, "No. We only make breakfast sandwiches."

Later I would learn that when Tom said no, the Stranger took a box of pancake mix off the shelf and handed it to Tom. He asked Tom to make pancakes anyway. "They're on me," he said. And so Tom did. And that is why the General Store makes pancakes now.

Tom brought out the second round of pancakes the Stranger had ordered. And the Stranger sat back down at the table. His afternoon plans were settled, but he still had to make plans for the evening. If we weren't all going to First Night, what *were* we doing?

We all wanted to tell him the truth. Tom, Brian, and me. I could feel it. But somehow we resisted. It was as if our astral selves consulted, joined hands in a circle, and cast a spell of protection.

"Nothing," we said. "Nothing at all. We're all getting older. No big plans. Probably we will each go back to our homes to stare at the wall in silence as the one year turns into the next."

We definitely did not say that in fact we were all going over to Heidi's house, along with most of the rest of the town and their children, to drink and play the party game called Mafia. We kept that quiet.

But then Heidi came into the store. She and her family were planning to join us on the sleigh ride, and she wanted to confirm the details.

As Tom had done for me, now I took her aside to warn her: *The Stranger is here! And also he is some kind of dark wizard who has captured our wills. He wanders as he pleases through our world, defies the rules of Maine, and makes Tom make him pancakes. I do not know why we are all still sitting here with him. I am not sure we are allowed to leave. I think Tom may have to make pancakes forever or else he will magically burst into flames like a scallop!*

I didn't warn her not to mention her party. I didn't think I had to. But Heidi is the sort of person who considers making friends with a dark wizard as a fun challenge. Or maybe she was just being neighborly where we had failed. She sat down and introduced herself. "I am having a party tonight," she said. "Come to my house."

The Stranger did not hesitate. He said yes. He just might.

And like that, the spell broke, and we were released.

BEFORE THE SLEIGH RIDE, we went home to collect our blankets and many layers. It was afternoon now, and afternoons blink away quickly to darkness in the winter in Maine. The temperature had already dropped to –2 degrees. We wondered if it was even safe to take a sleigh ride in this weather. But we didn't want to blow it off, because no matter what, Heidi would go anyway and then we would feel like weaklings.

Our daughter and Fiona joined us. As we drove over the peninsula, Fiona told us of her own encounter with the Stranger. It had happened earlier that day, before my wife and I got there, I think even before Tom was told to make pancakes. The Stranger spotted her at the register. They had a conversation. "He was just being friendly," she said. "But, for some reason, I felt like I was going to cry."

We arrived at Curtis's farm and met Heidi and her husband and kids. Curtis is in his early thirties, all height and shoulders and smiles. He stood out in the snow with Mike and Skid, the Belgian draft horses, both the color of cream soda. He was hooking them up to the sleigh using ropes or whatever. I do not know about these things, and Curtis didn't care that I didn't. He waved. It did not feel like –2 degrees around him.

As I had tried to explain to the Stranger, we had only known Curtis for a week. We had bought a last-minute tree from him when we arrived in town on Christmas Eve. We felt terrible about pulling him out of his house on Christmas Eve, but he didn't mind. He and his wife had only just purchased the farm, he explained, and they were trying to get the tree and sleigh ride business going. That made sense, but it did not explain why he sold us the tree for twenty dollars and then drove it twenty-five minutes to our house for free in his truck.

It also turns out that Fiona's mother had been his teacher when he was in grade school.

"Don't ask her about me!" he said. "I was a terror." This seemed very difficult to believe, and Fiona's mom later confirmed that he was not a terror at all. Of course he agreed to give the Stranger a sleigh ride, I realized. Curtis is a mutant Mainer who is actually very nice and who likes to work on Christmas Eve and give rides to strangers! Or maybe *I* was the one who didn't understand the rules of Maine.

Now we were bundled on the back of the sleigh: a newish wooden wagon perched atop a much older base, a twist of lumber and iron runners that looked to be a hundred years old.

"Don't worry," said Curtis. "It won't tip!" And we were off.

The cold gnawed at our faces. Mike and Skid trudged gamely. We asked Fiona to tell her story to Heidi, and she did.

The Stranger had come in and had spotted her behind the register. He smiled. He asked her if she ever cleaned house. The answer was yes. Fiona was growing up in Maine. Her father built boats and owned one. She could rig a sailboat and row a rowboat and haul cargo in and out of their lobster boat and catch moorings and tie knots. Her mother would sometimes rent out her own childhood home. In that house and in her own, Fiona was expected to help, and did so with no complaints and extreme competence.

As you might expect, I think my children are great. My daughter is smart and capable and good. But even she would admit, I think, that she is lazy compared to Fiona. So yes, Fiona had done everything. Yes, she had cleaned house. Had she changed bed linens? the Stranger asked. Yes, she had. Had she cleaned bathrooms? Yes. Toilets? Yes.

The Stranger was happy to hear this about Fiona. He told her he had purchased the house that used to belong to the Famous Author, and he needed someone to clean it.

The Stranger said, *You're hired.*

Fiona explained to him that she had to go to high school, so she did not have time to clean his house.

The things she didn't say to him, or even to us now as we rode through the bright and silent cold air on the sleigh, was that she maybe just didn't want to clean house for a summer person. That maybe she didn't like having to recite her résumé of hard and humble tasks, the things she does without a second thought, just to help her own family, and then to have those tasks hang in the air in front of her and see them fresh and remember that they are also the chores of a housekeeper. That maybe it isn't always fun to tell a stranger that, yes, you clean toilets. I thought maybe she didn't like being pulled off the shelf like a box of pancake mix.

It did not occur to her to say those things, and maybe she didn't even think them. She just told us her eyes had filled up with tears, but she didn't know why. And now in the sleigh, she laughed it off. "He was just trying to be nice in his own way," she said.

Mike's and Skid's hooves crunched the snow, and that was the only sound for a while. The sleigh turned at the top of the hill, and we saw a view straight across the woods, straight across the bay, all the way to Cadillac Mountain in Acadia National Park. We didn't know you could see Cadillac from here. It gave us something else to talk about.

Then, despite all promises, the sleigh tipped. On a turn back toward the barn, the right side of the sleigh, and those seated on it, pitched queasily upward. Those seated on the left side fell low into shadow. We made all kinds of noises. Curtis whoa'd Mike and Skid to a stop and the sleigh righted, but was still tippy and wrong-feeling. We got off it in quiet, gingerly panic, as if a single bad footfall would cause it to explode.

When Curtis got down to look under the sleigh, he saw that

a massive rod of iron that had supported the undercarriage had snapped in two.

"How did that even *happen*?" Curtis said.

Again, I'm no sleigh expert, but I am a writer, and I know a cliché when I see one. Some strange power in the universe had reached across dimensions to destroy Curtis's sleigh. A *deus* had literally fucked up his *machina* and snapped an ancient piece of iron impossibly in half because it had decided that there would be no more sleigh rides today.

Curtis was upset. He was going to have to tell the next guy he could not have a ride after all.

"Is his name the Stranger?" I asked, using the Stranger's actual name.

"That's right," Curtis said.

"I am the one who gave him your number," I told him. "But I need you to know, I don't really know him."

The snap of the sleigh snapped our mood too, and it was pleasant to walk down the hill. The air was cold but the sun was high. We had seen Cadillac Mountain by surprise and we had tipped but did not die. We remembered why we had ventured out in the dangerous cold: Maine only shows itself to those who do.

As we reached the bottom of the hill, Heidi said, "I'm going to have to talk to him." She said it as much to herself as to us, like acknowledging a dread chore, a New Year's resolution. "If he comes to my party, I have to explain to him. How he cannot be this way in this small town."

I have no doubt she *would* have done it. But I will spoil the story for you: she did not have to say it. He didn't show.

WE GATHERED THAT NIGHT at Heidi's. It was a big group, and we had fun. But even those who had not been at Mandatory Pancake Hour that morning felt quietly wary. By now the Stranger had been wandering around town the entire day. Many had encountered him. Inside it was bright and cheery and warm, but outside was dark, and doors didn't feel like much protection anymore.

Some people at the party were playing the game Mafia. I don't know if you have played Mafia. It is also known as Werewolf. It is a party game for those who are not content to stand in the kitchen drinking and talking about television shows and movies like normal people.

I do not play Mafia, obviously. But the game play is more or less like this: The group of players forms a village. They are randomly assigned roles. Some are innocent villagers, others are mafiosi, or werewolves, or some other horror that creeps among us unseen by day, but by night comes to murder one person each evening. A moderator leads the play. The moderator leads the villagers through the day, where they each try to guess who is the horror. Then the moderator leads them through the night, where the villagers must close their eyes and wait for the horror to come and take them. This was precisely our mood.

At one moment, when I was busy shoving food into my face

and not playing Mafia, a neighbor I will not name took me aside and into their confidence. They told me their own story of the Stranger. It was a version of the stories everyone had been telling that night, about the thing the Stranger said, the personal questions he asked, the demands he made, the confessions he pulled from us, the private places he went, both physical and emotional, in cheerful ease, and the uncanny feeling that we could not stop him. This person's story was routine by now. But this person, one of the sweetest people I know, couldn't shake it. They said, "I can't believe I'm saying this, but do we need to... *eliminate* him?"

Now, this person did not mean it literally. They had just been eliminated from the game of Mafia themselves, so it was on their mind. So let me assure you, reader, that no harm will come to the Stranger. I don't need to assure the Stranger about this, as things in town have changed.

I know this because I have spent a little time with the Stranger since that New Year's Eve. I saw him once last spring, a few times last summer. And each time, he makes a point of saying he has my book, but he has not read it yet. But he seems very happy to have it, and I can't help but like that. He reminds me that he owns the Famous Author's house and invites me to come see it. He offers to send me the screenplay he's writing. And I say yes, sure. But he never actually sends it to me, which is a special kind of kindness.

The most recent time I saw him, I was making breakfast sandwiches. There was something new at the Store: a swinging saloon-style half-door at the kitchen entryway. It had a sign on it that read "Employees Only." Obviously, this rule was a lie. It was just me and Tom working in the kitchen that morning, and neither of us are employees.

But in small towns, we have to find ways to get along. We conjure imaginary boundaries and eventually respect them. And the Stranger has come to actually respect the imaginary boundary that was conjured to keep him out. That morning, as I was drawing mayonnaise *J*s on the English muffins, the Stranger popped his head above the swinging door with a smile.

"Tom! They said they put this in for insurance reasons," the Stranger said. "But I know it was because of me!" He said it proudly. It made him happy to be part of the town.

"That's probably right!" Tom said as he made the Stranger's pancakes.

The warmth in their back-and-forth was obvious. He and Tom had formed an actual bond, and it had happened when I was away. He had probably spent more time in town than I had that year.

Later I would learn that the Stranger had read *Atlas Shrugged* but was not a Ayn Rand adherent. I would learn that he didn't mean to *order* Tom to make pancakes. He doesn't get to see his kids as much as he likes, but he had convinced them to visit for Christmas in part on the promise of blueberry pancakes. When he learned the Store didn't serve them, he panicked. He asked Tom to make them, and Tom had done the Stranger an enormous favor. And in fact, Tom still makes blueberry pancakes on Sundays, expanding the Stranger's legacy in the Store. He certainly didn't mean to make Fiona almost feel like crying.

"I have a big personality," the Stranger told me. "I'm outgoing. I know this. Sometimes I forget that people don't automatically know my good intentions."

I know this because I spoke to the Stranger after I sent him this story. I had to let him read it, of course, or else I would be a real-life monster. I can't imagine it was easy to read. But he did it, and responded thoughtfully and generously, with no defensiveness. Yes, he is a little tone-deaf and he probably does live on the far other end of the political spectrum from me. But I now know that Fiona was right all along: he was just trying to be friendly.

Later that morning I saw that the Stranger's wife had made a special order for cheesy scrambled eggs. I made it for her. I enjoyed doing it. Partly because we are neighbors, partly because I just really like making eggs. We are all villagers. We are all innocents and horrors. We close our eyes and have to trust one another.

THAT WAS LAST SUMMER. But in the winter, when we were huddled together against the New Year's Eve dark, I remembered something.

In my last book, I made a joke that maybe Maine was a death cult. My family and I had been outsiders when we arrived. We had come to town and felt observed and quietly tested. And if we failed the test, I wondered if we would be taken in the night and... *eliminated.*

Now, at Heidi's house, I learned that not only was my joke absolutely, almost literally true, but now I was on the other side of it. I was no longer the outsider. I had been allowed into the village, and here was the assistant fire chief and here were the owners of the Store where my daughter and I worked. Here were the generations of Fiona's family, the mother who had taught Curtis, the father who had inherited the boat that belonged to the woman who gave our road its name, the daughter who almost cried but didn't. Here was the owner of the boatyard, the grandson of the Famous Author (whose house the Stranger now owned). And now he knew my name, and I knew his.

But I won't tell his name to you because I'm trying to at least *pretend* to keep some confidences here. I'm trying to stay in this village, even though by revealing what I have, I may have already messed it up, maybe even hurt these people I care about. I have to do it. For one, it's a pretty good story, and I only have so much material. But also, I think there may be a better reason. Maybe to remind us to be good to each other, and especially to be good to people who work in stores and have to talk to you. Maybe to remind us to be good to people who haven't quite figured out the rules yet. Maybe to remind us that there are, per Tolstoy, only two stories. A person goes on a journey. And a stranger comes to town. But if you *are* the stranger, those two stories are the same.

(Someone go dig Tolstoy up and tell him he missed a step,

dummy. But don't worry, Hodgman's got it: we all journey as strangers.)

As midnight approached, the grandson of the Famous Author got eliminated from the game. He had been accused of being the horror—wrongly, if I remember correctly—but he seemed happy about it. He found me in the kitchen. We watched the remaining players bicker with one another while the moderator yelled for silence.

"I don't see the appeal of this game," he said. "Why not just hang out here in the kitchen?"

"I absolutely agree with you, person who knows my name!" I said. I told him I was going to make a martini, and I offered to make him one, and he said yes, and I was never more excited in my life to provide this service.

As someone who had once been a little bit famous, I had been invited into a number of private clubs and hidden worlds, sky lounges and secret societies, real and figurative. But when the Stranger had asked me what I did for a living, I had no answer. Because on some level, I belonged to *this* secret society now, of being here and making eggs. The other world I described in this book felt far behind me.

We drank our martinis. Someone in the game stalked off in anger, someone laughed. Soon there would be fireworks down by the boatyard. As midnight neared, the spell of fear and anxiety broke. If the Stranger had walked in at that moment, he would have been welcome.

Acknowledgments

This book was harder to write than the last one. Sometime in the 1990s, when I knew Elizabeth Gilbert and you probably didn't yet, Liz asked me, "Why do you write?"

I said I didn't know.

I don't enjoy writing. It's always a moment of nauseating panic to look into my head for ideas, because (a) nobody asked for them, and (b) what if there are none left? I will do almost anything to avoid writing, as the career path recounted in this book will prove. However, this *book* also exists, which proves what I told Liz back then, with resignation: I write because, for some reason, I can't not.

"Why do *you* write, Liz?" I asked.

"Oh," she said. "I guess because it's easy and fun!"

I love Liz so much. She is an amazing friend and a deeply inspiring artist and human. But I really hated her that day.

But then *Vacationland* came along, and for the first time ever writing was easy and fun! I looked forward to sitting down every day and watching casually as my hands typed out the words in perfect order, everything right the first time, every time. I enjoyed it so much I immediately asked Brian Tart at Viking if I could write another book, and he said yes, and I said thank you and looked forward to another year of fun ease.

But it didn't happen that way. It turned out that writing this book was hard and nauseating, just like always! I had forgotten that, by the time I had sat down to write *Vacationland*, I had already stood up and told most of those stories countless times onstage. They had been pre-drafted and honed and corrected, the panicky nausea of starting them masked long before by butterflies and pre-show whiskey at Union Hall.

Now I had to start from the hard, blank beginning again, and so I remembered the lesson a somewhat more foul-mouthed advisor than Liz had told me once: your brain won't let you fuck up. Kenny Shopsin told me that at his restaurant almost ten years ago when I was facing down my deadline for *That Is All*. And I've come to learn what he meant over time: the hard part is starting. That's the moment when you are utterly convinced that there is nothing left in your memory worth remembering, never mind telling. But once you start moving your fingers on the typewriter, even if you're just typing the plain dumb facts of what you did that day, your brain will stop being a stingy asshole, as Kenny might say, and start offering you those flashes of memory and connection that form stories.

Stories are a survival technique: they are how we put our lives and universe into some consoling order. That's why I can't not write, and even if *you* don't actually write on paper, *you* can't not write either. Your brain is always writing, cataloguing and shaping the narrative of your life, because it wants to survive too. And if it's a matter of life or death or a deadline, it won't let you fuck up. With a push, your brain will show you the stories you've been telling yourself all along, both the terrible lies and the surprising truths. (This is also why therapy works.)

I can't describe the depth of feeling that inhabits me when I finally see the true story that my brain has been hiding from me, the one I would have never thought about or even *known* if I hadn't bothered to start writing. Revelation, I guess. Anyway, it's a good feeling, and I guess that's why I write, Liz.

Kenny Shopsin died last August. I'm glad I got to thank him often for his advice while he was alive, but I'll just start by saying thank you once more, in writing this time.

Here are some other people who made this book a little easier, or at least a little possible. Ken Plume is not only my friend, but my memory, and I am grateful to him for rereading my old books and remembering the stories I've already told.

Thank you to all my fake friends and families on television: Paul and Jamie and Brett and Judy and Nat and Jenny and Sarah and Ennis and Richard and Alexandra and Craig and Josh and Annabelle and Griffin and Peter and Yara and Scott and Brendan and Sir Patrick and Lola and all my good guy friends on the *Blindspot* good guy squad. Thank you, Eric, for suggesting that we rehearse our dinner scene and bringing a chicken to my house to do so. Thank you to my murderers Jamie and Maya. I know you did what you had to.

Thank you Martin and Andrew and Joe and Gregory and Jack and Michael and Stephen and Carmen and Jonathan and Roman and Jason and Ben and Jackson and Swampy and Pendleton and Jon, for putting me in your worlds. Thank you Jamie, for making me be better, and thank you, Halley, for making me cry.

Thank you to Lindsay and all the second ADs who moved me into place, as well as all the first ADs, PAs, HMU department heads and staff, camera operators, wardrobers, property masters, lighters and gaffers and best boys and soundies and crafties and everyone else who, on every working set, has so consistently blown me away with your graciousness and professionalism and humor, even in the middle of the night in a waste processing plant. I'm sorry I almost never could remember everyone's names. Set life for life.

Thank you to my whole team at UTA, and I mean that sincerely, but now the orchestra is playing me off, so let me wrap this up by saying thank you as always to Brian Tart for letting me do this again, to Kassie Evashevski for expertly guiding me and this book home to Viking, to everyone at Viking for making it real, and to Aaron Draplin for making it beautiful.

I think it's fair to say that two people utterly changed my life and sent me on this unlikely journey toward minor fame and medallion status. Unlike Kenny, I didn't get to thank one of them before he was gone. The other I've thanked countless times, but he swats thank-yous away like they were disgusting, fat flies. But I'll just say here: Thank you, Steve, and thank you, Jon. I'm sorry I fucked up and stayed home that day when you were looking for me in the office.

Finally, thank you and thank you again, Elizabeth Gilbert, for always counseling me to do the right thing, even when it is not easy. And on the same subject, thank you to all of my neighbors in Maine, old and new, for their trust and inspiring decency.

Double finally and always: thank you to Katherine, Lucy, and James. The sun is still warm. I love you.

That is all.